# The Living Atlas

Fraser Cartwright
Jim Gilchrist

with illustrations by
David Shaw

**gage** EDUCATIONAL PUBLISHING COMPANY
A DIVISION OF CANADA PUBLISHING CORPORATION
TORONTO ONTARIO CANADA

# Introduction

**Canadian Cataloguing in Publication Data**

Cartwright, Fraser, 1947–
    The living atlas

ISBN 0-7715-8168-8

1. Maps — Juvenile literature.   2. Maps — Problems, exercises, etc. — Juvenile literature.   3. Cartography — Juvenile literature.   4. Cartography — Problems, exercises, etc. — Juvenile literature.   5. Canada — Maps — Juvenile literature.   6. Canada — Maps — Problems, exercises, etc. — Juvenile literature. I. Gilchrist, Jim, 1940–    .  II. Shaw, David, 1947–    .  III. Title.

GA130.C37   1990     912′.014     C90-094336-X

Design: David Shaw

**Photo Credits**
Aquarius Flight Inc., 27; Courtesy of West Edmonton Mall, 30–31; Image courtesy of the Canada Centre for Remote Sensing, Energy, Mines and Resources Canada, 37; Aquarius Flight Inc., 49; The Province of British Columbia, (Vancouver Trade and Convention Centre) 57; Aerial photography produced courtesy of Ministry of Crown Lands, Surveys and Resource Mapping Branch, Government of British Columbia, 57; Robert B. Mansour Limited, 58; Gabe Ascenzo, 62; Courtesy of the Embassy of Japan, 64 top left; Robert B. Mansour Limited, 64 top right; New Zealand High Commission, 64 bottom left; Courtesy of Air Canada, (Air Canada plane) 65; British Tourist Authority, (Tower Bridge) 65; Property of Moscow-MacDonald's, (MacDonald's in Red Square) 65; Courtesy of Paris Opera House, (Paris Opera House) 65.

ISBN: 0-7715-8168-8

1 2 3 4 5 6 7 8   FP   97 96 95 94 93 92 91 90

Written, printed, and bound in Canada

*The Living Atlas* presents an innovative and exciting method of introducing children 9 to 12 years of age to the following basic map understandings:

- **View:** the view of features shown on maps is from above (top-down perspective).
- **Spacing:** all features on a map have a spatial relationship or connection with all other map features.
- **Symbolic language:** when shapes and colors are used on a map to represent real-life features they become the "language" of the map.
- **Size and distance:** maps show areas and features that are usually smaller than real life or actual size.
- **Direction:** the spatial relationships of features on a map can be described by the use of words and cardinal points.
- **Referencing:** the location of features on a map may be given by using a grid.
- **Application:** a map becomes real for users when they develop an ability to understand and apply its message.

Each page identifies the map understanding which is being developed. These understandings are expanded through levels of difficulty which are appropriate for children aged 9 to 12 years.

Although no divisions appear in *The Living Atlas*, it could be considered to be divided into several sections:

## Pages 1 to 31

These pages guide the user through experiences that systematically introduce and develop basic map understandings in a friendly, engaging, and interactive way. Organizers are used creatively to develop concepts. *Globug*, a bug representing the globe and all peoples, is used throughout the atlas. In the early pages of the atlas, Globug works with the child and becomes involved in the activities. In later pages, Globug appears only in the illustrations.

## Pages 32 to 36

These are the transitional pages. They lead the child from basic map understandings to more opportunities to **make** maps. The central skill of mapping by **observation** is developed by using the child's immediate environment. The skills are then applied to an area much larger than a child would be able to verify visually in real life. This move towards more abstract understanding and interpretation is helped by the friendly and humorous illustrations of David Shaw.

## Pages 37 to 54

In these pages, thematic maps of Canada are introduced. Again, these are very illustrative and interactive. The student becomes comfortable with abstract mapping and gains a knowledge of the geography of Canada.

## Pages 55 to 63

Maps on these pages allow the child to become familiar with the location and character of Canadian regions. Page 55 explains the purpose of a gazetteer. Maps on pages 56 to 67 are referenced in the gazetteer.

## Pages 64 to 67

These pages introduce the child to Canada and its relationship to the rest of the world. Global maps of the world are used as the child becomes familiar with the more abstract and traditional map.

As an outcome, the use of *The Living Atlas* enables the child to understand the fundamentals of maps. Through a variety of different learning experiences, we believe the child will develop the skills necessary to apply meaningfully all maps to the real world they represent and appreciate this ability as a life skill.

It is through our work with maps and children over many years that we are confident children will enjoy this unique and exciting introduction to maps. We would like to thank and congratulate David Shaw for his wonderful illustrations that have helped to make our ideas come alive.

**Note:** Most thematic/reference maps are drawn with an oblique view. The approximate distances on the line scales are appropriate only at a similar horizontal level. Distances further north or south of the line scale are therefore distorted.

# Table of Contents

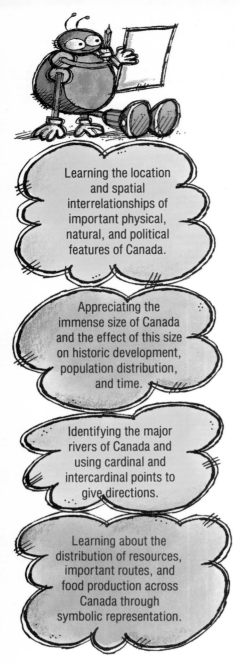

Learning the location and spatial interrelationships of important physical, natural, and political features of Canada.

Appreciating the immense size of Canada and the effect of this size on historic development, population distribution, and time.

Identifying the major rivers of Canada and using cardinal and intercardinal points to give directions.

Learning about the distribution of resources, important routes, and food production across Canada through symbolic representation.

Applying knowledge and skills acquired in previous units while learning about weather patterns, environmental issues, and sport patterns.

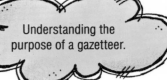

Understanding the purpose of a gazetteer.

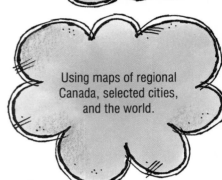

Using maps of regional Canada, selected cities, and the world.

### Dedication

We would like to dedicate this atlas to several very special people:

Fraser's children, **Jeffrey** and **Johnathan**, who were an inspiration throughout the development of the manuscript and to whom *Globug* became a real person. Also to **Bonnie**, Fraser's wife, for ongoing encouragement and support.

Jim's longtime friend and mentor, **Björn Kjellström**, who introduced the sport of orienteering to Canada in 1948. He provided the inspiration, leadership, and support for thousands of Canadian and American children and adults to learn how to use a map and compass. In doing this, he taught us a way to enjoy the outdoors.

### Acknowledgments

Our thanks to the students and teachers of York Region who were the inspiration for many of the ideas and concepts fundamental to this atlas. Also to Helene Huculak who has helped to make maps, compasses, and orienteering an important part of Jim's life since 1970; Cathy Cripps who assisted with the editing and whose resourcefulness and patience led to so much of the support material we needed for the book; Anne Marie Moro whose energy, enthusiasm, and unwavering commitment to the vision of a different kind of atlas for children got the project off the ground; and to Sylvia Gilchrist, the principal editor, who inspired, encouraged, cajoled, forgave, and made suggestions to us in order to keep the project flying and, finally, to bring it home.

# A Bug with a View

Have you ever noticed how the shape of some things seems to change when you look at or **view** them from different sides or angles?

Look at the shapes in the boxes around Globug. There are *eight* boxes but only *four* different objects. What are the four objects? There are two views of each object. Match them up.

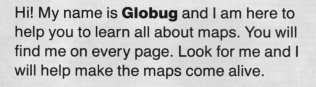

Hi! My name is **Globug** and I am here to help you to learn all about maps. You will find me on every page. Look for me and I will help make the maps come alive.

Any object can look different or appear to have a different shape when seen from various angles or views.

Take off one shoe and trace the outline of its sole on a piece of paper.

Inside the outline list only the names of the parts of the shoe that you can see when you look at it from above. Can you see the front, the back, and the sides? If so, don't forget to list them.

Now draw an outline of your shoe looking at it from one side. Inside the outline print only the names of the parts of the shoe that you can see from this view.

Which view allows you to see the most parts of the shoe?

Imagine you are in the following situations:
● riding a bicycle on a new street
● playing a game of soccer
● lost in a shopping mall

How would it help if you could see the street, the soccer field, and the mall from above?

# A Bird's-eye View

Globug is taking a ride on the back of a bird and looking down on a village. From this view, Globug sees only the top of everything. This is a **view from above**. Sometimes this view is called a **bird's-eye** view. This is different from the view you have of the village in the picture. Name some of the things you can see.

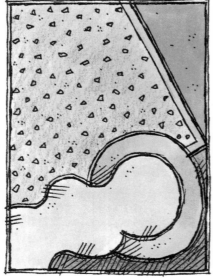

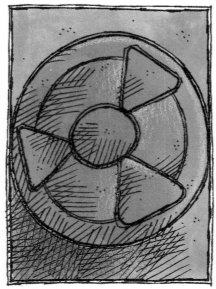

Here is Globug's bird's-eye view of seven objects. Find each of them in the village. What are they?

Imagine you are a bird flying over this village. Write a short story describing what you can see as you look down.

# Higher and Higher

Imagine you and Globug are in a hot air balloon looking down at a school which has its roof off. From this view from above, you can see all the classrooms.

Here is a closer look at one of the rooms. List some of the different activities you can see.

Build a model of the classroom in the picture. You will need a large sheet of paper and some building blocks. Work with two other people.

Use the paper to represent the floor and the blocks to represent the desks, shelves, couch, filing cabinet, and table. Use one block for each student desk and two blocks for the couch. How will you show the teacher's desk, which is larger than a student desk, and the shelves, which look like long rectangles?

Arrange the blocks on the paper in the same pattern as the objects they represent in the picture. Check your model from all sides until it looks right.

Make a record of your model by using a pencil to draw an outline around the blocks. Be careful not to move them. As each outline is completed, take the blocks away. How will you show what the shapes in your drawing represent once the blocks are removed?

Look at what others have done. Tell them what you like best about the record they have made of their models.

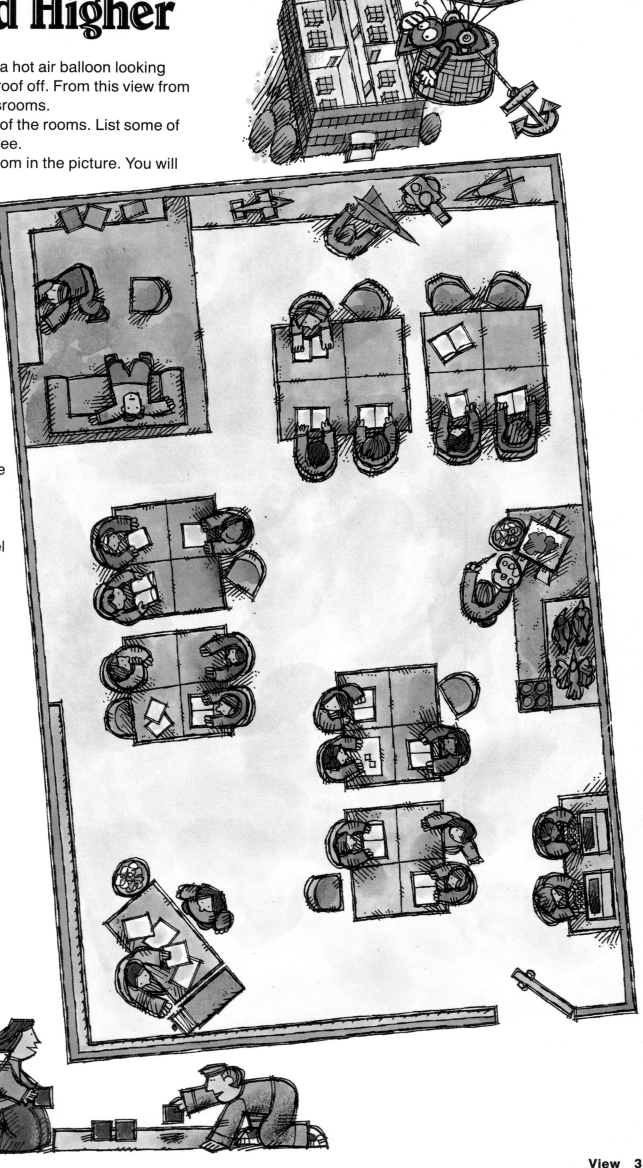

# Beside, Behind, Across...

Find Globug in this picture. Describe where Globug is standing. Use words such as *beside, across from, in front of*, and *near*.

You are learning to use **location words** to describe where something is in relation to the things around it. These words may also be used to give directions to a place.

Each day, Globug uses the same route to go to and from school. Globug passes stores, a playground, a gas station, a duck pond, and other interesting things. What do you pass on your way to school?

Copy the organizer. The items on the left are places that Globug passes to and from school. Find them in the picture and complete the chart. Follow the example for the donut shop. You can see that the donut shop has a number of items around it found by looking in different directions.

Play a game where one person thinks of a place and the other person discovers the location by asking questions using the location words above.

| places Globug passes | beside | across from | in front of | near |
|---|---|---|---|---|
| donut shop | barber | fountain and pond | house | school |
| pet store | | | | |
| playground | | | | |
| cinema | | | | |

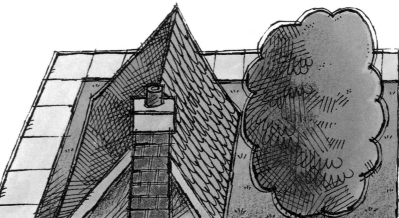

# Fun at the Fair

You are at the fair with Globug. What is in front of you as you stand at the entrance? Visit the *Flyer*. Describe its location using location words.

Walk to the pig pens. Stand facing the pigs in the middle of the pathway between the pens and Mme. Tina's booth. Name two places on your left and one on your right that you could visit.

From the pig pens, select a route to the ferris wheel. List the things you will see on your right and on your left as you walk to the ferris wheel. Give your list to a partner to see if he or she can discover the route you took. Enjoy your ride on the ferris wheel. Could it be confusing to use right and left when giving directions? Why?

After your ride, select a place you would like to visit. Write a simple description of how you would reach it from the ferris wheel. Ask someone to follow your description to find you.

Were there any problems in following your route? Discuss them.

Why is it important to be able to give easy-to-follow directions to find places? When have you given directions for people to follow?

# Big Bear, Little Bear

You are at the wax museum with Globug. Study the picture carefully. The models on display represent **real-life size**. This is the actual size the object is in real life.

Compare the size of the bear on display to the size of the bear Globug is holding. Name some things you have that are much smaller than real-life size; for example, do you have a toy car? What is the advantage in having items that are smaller than real-life size?

Make a list of all the items in the picture. Now rewrite your list in order of real-life size, from the smallest to the largest. Compare your list with someone else's list.

# Ready, Set, Climb...

Globug is timing and refereeing a pole climb. The poles have been drawn to fit on this page but in real-life size they are very tall.

Look at the ruler on the right for measuring distance. It is divided into metres. If you were 2 m up the pole in the picture, imagine what that would be like in real life. To find out, place a sticker on the wall 2 m up from the floor. Step back and look at that distance. That is how high you would be.

The ruler can be used to measure other parts of the pole. How tall are the poles? How far are the bells from the ground?

Play the following game with one or two others. You will need one die and a different marker for each climber. Decide the order for throwing the die. Each number rolled on the die represents the number of metres you may climb up the pole. Roll until you reach exactly 10 m. For example, if you are at 8 m, you must roll a 2 to get to 10 m. Before you can begin the climb down, you must ring the bell. To ring the bell you must roll a 6. Play until one climber finishes. The number you roll to finish must take you to zero or ground level.

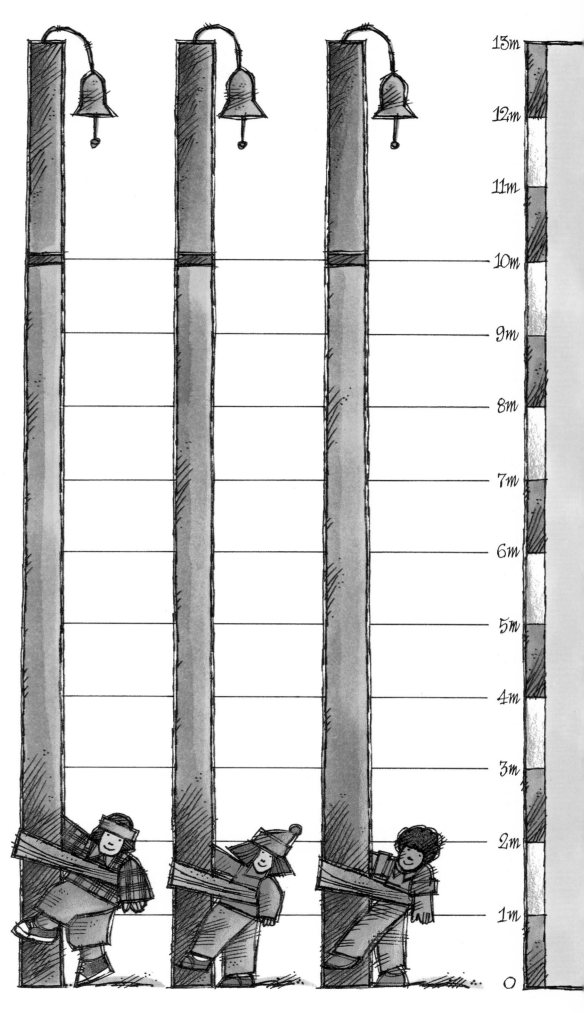

# Beastie Chase

When the game is over, calculate the total distance you have travelled. Could you have selected a shorter, safer route?

Here is another chance to try your skill at measuring distances.

Look at the ruler at the bottom of the page. This is a special ruler. It tells you how many metres in real-life distance are represented by each centimetre on the ruler. This type of ruler is called a **line scale**. How long is the whole line scale in real-life distance?

Trace the line scale and cut it out. Use it like a ruler to measure distance. Look at the *Beastie Chase* game. How many metres down from the start is the first dark square? Look at the second dark square across from the start. How far away would it be in real-life distance? How far would a bird fly from start to finish? If you have trouble using your line scale cutout, what else could you use? Try some other measurements.

Play the *Beastie Chase* game. You will need two different markers and one die. Your challenge is to see who can get through the *Land of the Beasties* the fastest.

Begin the game by putting your marker at the start. Roll the die. The person who rolls the highest number goes first. Roll again to find the number of squares to move. Every dark square is a beastie chase. If you land on one at the end of your move, you must go back 100 m. How many squares is that? If you land on a dark square two turns in a row, you have to miss a turn. Keep track of the metres you travel, forward and back. Each player must continue until he or she reaches the finish.

START

FINISH

0    50    100    150    200    250    300 m

1 cm represents 50m

# Bus Stop Bustle

There are many different ways to give direction. Some ways are more accurate than others. You have already used words and phrases such as *beside, across from, in front of, near, left, right*. You have also learned that using these words can sometimes confuse people. There is a more accurate method.

Look at the drawing of the compass. It shows the four **cardinal points:** *north, south, east, west*. A picture has been drawn opposite each point illustrating what some people think of when they have to travel in these directions. What picture do you think of for each of the cardinal points?

One advantage to using cardinal points when giving directions is that they are the same all over the world. For example, if you asked a friend in Japan and another friend in France to walk east, they would walk in the same direction as you if you also walked east.

Another advantage is that you need only to know the direction of one of the cardinal points to know the other three. Why is that?

Study the picture of the streets. In the top right corner you will find Globug driving a school bus. Children are waiting on street corners to be picked up. Give Globug directions using the cardinal points and street names to pick up the children.

Dogwood Ave.

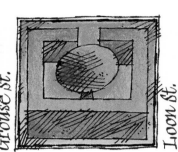

Crocus Ave.

Owl St.

Grouse St.

Loon St.

Chickadee St.

Lily Ave.

Mayflower Ave.

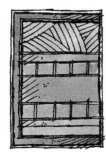

Pitcher Plant Ave.

# Winter Adventure

This winter adventure will give you practice in following the directions of the cardinal points. It will also give you a chance to learn something about how to take care of yourself in the cold outdoors. Follow the directions below.

- You are dressed and ready for an afternoon of cross-country skiing with your parents. List some of the things you think you should carry in a small backpack to help make the outing safer. You will begin at the cottage.
- From "C," the cottage, ski 5 spaces north to where the trail bends to the east.

- Check the map and compass for direction. Ski 10 spaces east.
- You are feeling hot. Open your ski jacket. Ski 3 spaces south.
- Check the time. It is one o'clock and you have been gone one hour. Ski 4 spaces east.
- You are at a stream but the ice looks thin. Ice is often thin on streams. Detour 8 spaces north.
- Check the map and compass. You are not sure where you are. In what direction was your last stop? Check the compass and ski 7 spaces west.
- You are starting to feel cold because you are getting tired. What do you have in your backpack to help you warm up? Ski 4 spaces west.

- Detour 2 spaces south around a large hill.
- Rest. It is three o'clock and getting late. You must be close to one of two trails which run directly to the cottage.
- Using cardinal points, plan the remainder of the trip to the cottage following a route of your choice.

Did you have in your backpack the things you needed? What were some of the other items you included and why do you think they are important?

# Follow That Sign

Here are a number of traffic signs. There are no words on the signs but people who drive cars or ride bicycles on the street must understand and obey some of them. All the signs use pictures so that they can be understood by people who speak any language. Pictures used this way are called **symbols**.

What is the symbol on each sign telling you? The meaning for each can be found in the lists on the right. Match the correct meaning to each sign.

Airport
Signals Ahead
Deer Crossing
School Area
Stop Ahead

Do Not Enter
Food
Hospital
Slippery When Wet
Camping

Imagine that you are in charge of inventing new symbols for traffic signs. Draw two or three. Ask someone else to guess the meaning.

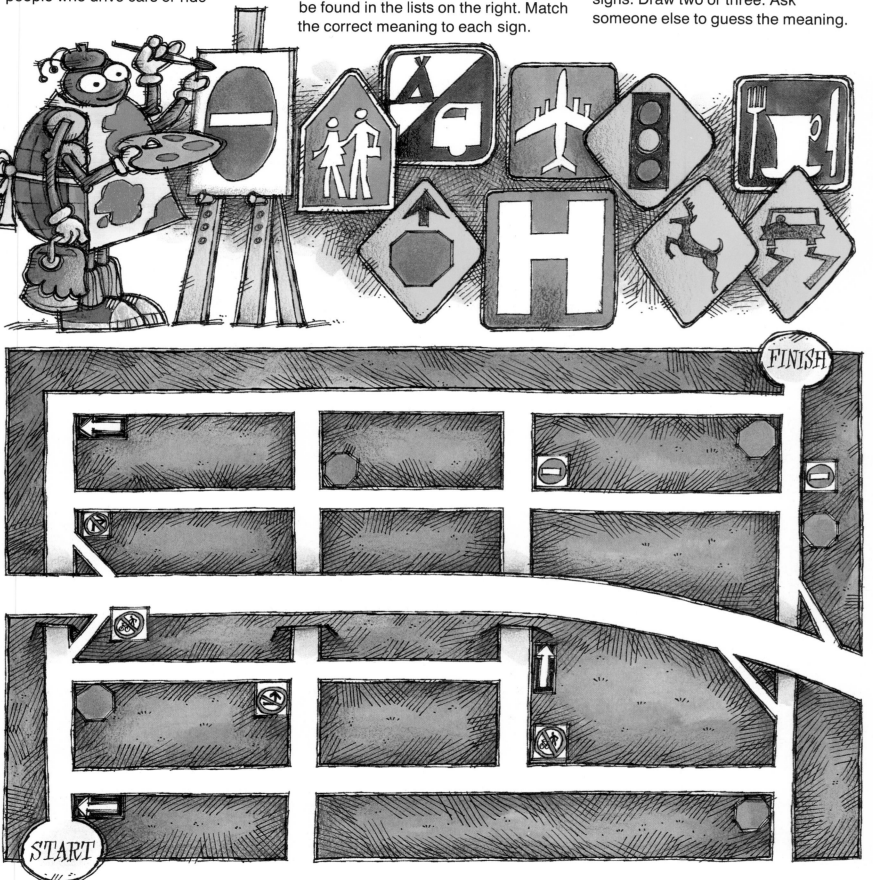

You are going to take an imaginary street riding test on your bicycle. You have to get from the start to the finish. All traffic signs must be obeyed in the same way that you would if you were really out on the road. If you arrive at an intersection and there is no sign you may go in a direction of your choice.

Work with a partner and say what you are doing as you ride along.

Explain the meaning of each traffic sign you come to on your way to the finish. Remember to obey all signs. You will receive a ticket each time you break the law.

# Paint That Symbol

Look at the stores in the top plaza. The service provided by each store is indicated by a symbol. What does each store sell?

The symbols for each store in the bottom plaza have not been made. Help Globug by creating symbols that identify the service provided by each store.

Can others understand your symbols? Make whatever changes you feel are necessary to improve the message of your symbols.

# Flames in the Dump

Emergency! Fire! Globug has just received a call at the fire station that the dump is on fire and the fire may spread to the forest. Globug would like you to plan the quickest and safest route to the fire. Even though it is an emergency, all traffic laws must be obeyed. You also have to pick up four volunteer firefighters on the way. They have heard the alarm and are waiting to be picked up.

Make sure you plan carefully the route to the fire. More than one route is possible. Use the line scale at the bottom of the picture to compare distances. Remember that many turns will slow you down. The shortest route may not be the fastest.

To make sure that you do not forget which way to go, write down the directions you will give Globug.

Don't forget to pick up the volunteer firefighters.

Exchange your directions with someone else. Discuss any problems in understanding them.

# Upstairs or Downstairs

Words and symbols are not always enough when you need directions to find things. Here is another way to give directions to find places.

The string around the parcel Globug is holding divides the package into four sections. What is the easiest way to describe the location of the stamps? If you are using words like *right* and *upper*, you have the idea.

How would you state the location of the addresses and the "fragile" sticker?

It is easy when the area is divided into only four parts. How would you state a location if there were many parts? Study the apartment building on the right. The apartments form a pattern of squares. This pattern of squares is called a **grid**. A grid may be used to help you find places. There are numbers for each floor on the sides and letters for each row of apartments along the top and bottom. To find an apartment, first give its letter from the top or bottom and then its number from either one of the sides.

Use the letters and numbers on the grid to answer the following questions:

- Where does Globug live? (*answer: B2*)
- Which three apartments will be affected most by the noisy guitar player?
- What color are the curtains in the apartment above A7?
- In which apartment can you see the most children?
- Which apartment gets flooded when the bath in B7 overflows?
- Which apartments have a dog?

Try some of your own questions with another person.

# Washed Ashore

Shipwreck! Globug's ship hit a coral reef in the South Pacific and sank. Fortunately, you and the crew are all good swimmers and are now safe on this island. You may need to stay for a few months so you will have to build a shelter and find food and water.

Your first task is to make a record of what is on the island. Prepare lists of *natural* and *washed ashore* items. *Natural* means things that have always been part of the island. *Washed ashore* means things from your ship.

Study the lists carefully. What items are essential for your survival? Discuss each item and its importance to survival very carefully. Your life could depend upon your decisions.

Copy the organizer. In the left column write, in order of importance, the ten items essential to your survival.

To help Globug organize the crew, you need to include on your organizer the grid letters and numbers necessary to find the items. These are called **grid references**. You will also need to indicate the distance from camp to each item. Camp is where the shirt is flying like a flag. Use the line scale to measure the distance to each item.

| Survival Items | Grid Reference | Distance |
|---|---|---|
|  |  |  |
|  |  |  |

1 cm represents 100 m

# Mapping a Classroom

You are now going to apply what you have learned to make a map of a classroom.

Look at the drawing of the classroom on this page. What is this view of the classroom called? Where are you to have this view?

To help you to make your finished drawing or map as accurate as possible, follow these steps.

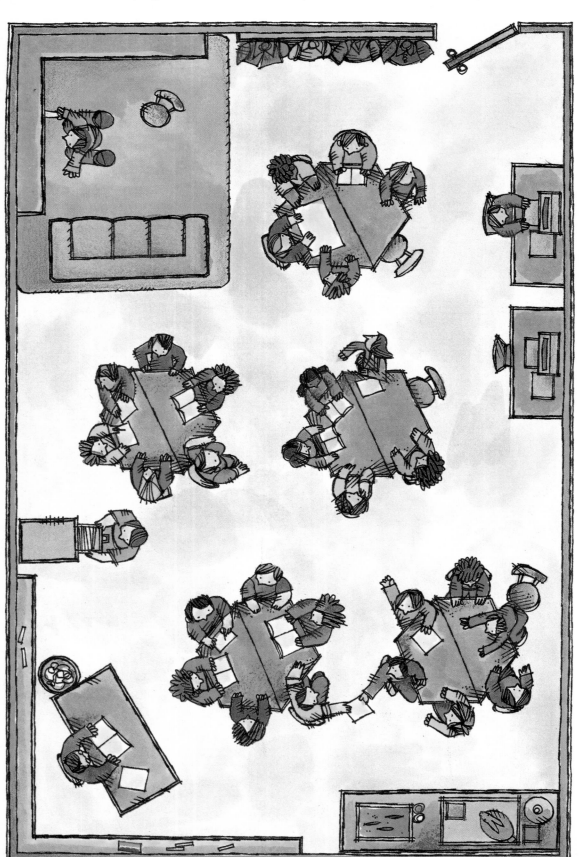

### 1/Prepare an Inventory

Make a list of all the things or **features** that you want on your map. This list is called an **inventory**. Make a copy of the organizer to help you get started. It is not necessary to list everything you see in the classroom. Choose features that can be seen from above and which seldom or never change their location in the room. Remember, your finished map will tell a story of the classroom and that story should be accurate for a long time.

| symbols | features |
|---|---|
| | doorway |
| | desk |
| | couch |

### 2/Create a Legend

Create symbols to represent each of the features. This must be done with care because the symbols will become the language of the map. The following will help you to create your symbols:

- The shape of the symbol should be the same as the main shape of the feature when viewed from above (e.g. a *rectangle* for teacher's desk).
- There must be a different symbol for each feature.
- Symbols should be simple and easy to draw.

When the organizer showing a symbol for each feature is complete, you will have created a **legend**. All maps should have a legend because the legend is the language which allows you to understand the map.

| symbols | features |
|---|---|
| —⊢⊢— | doorway |
| ▭ | desk |
| | couch |

## 3/Draw a Frame

With your legend, you are now ready to draw a map. It will become a story of the classroom told in your language using symbols. It is important to begin the drawing with a **frame**. For a classroom the frame is usually made up of the walls and a doorway. One or two features in the room may be added as reference points. On a sheet of paper, make a frame similar to the one on the right. Remember to leave room for the legend.

## 4/Fit the Map

When your frame is completed, place it beside the picture of the classroom so that the doorway and features in the frame are in the same place as the ones in the picture. This is called **fitting** the frame to the picture. Fitting the frame or finished map to the place it represents is important for many reasons as you will discover in your work with other maps in this atlas.

LEGEND

| ⊣ ⊢ | doorway | | |
|---|---|---|---|
| ▭ | desk | | |
| | couch | | |
| | | | |

## 5/Add Features

The first features to add to the frame are the ones against the wall. Decide from the picture where you want to begin and find that place in the frame. Be careful to make sure that the size and spacing of your symbols match the features in the picture. As you draw, keep your map fitted at all times. It will help you to be more accurate and to avoid mistakes. You will make some errors, so draw very lightly with your pencil until everything is the way it should be.

Move along each of the four walls adding features from your legend. They have to be placed accurately because they will be used to help you find the correct location of things in the rest of the room. Check your fitted map frequently with the picture.

Return to your starting position near the wall and begin adding the remaining symbols. Look at the rest of the room. Make sure your map is fitted when you draw. Add symbols for the features nearest you. Continue doing this at different places along all four walls. Make sure that each new symbol lines up with the symbols along the wall in the same way as in the picture. When you have finished, check to see that everything is properly spaced in terms of *behind, beside, in front of*. . . .

## 6/Check the Accuracy

Plan an imaginary walk in the picture and then try the same walk on your map. If you bump into furniture, check the spacing and/or size of your symbols again. Once you are satisfied with your drawing, go over all your work with a dark pencil.

Congratulations! You have successfully completed a difficult task using a step-by-step plan. You can follow the same steps to draw maps of much larger places.

# Mapping the Inside of a School

The frame on the right is a view from above of the hallways and walls of a school. The location of classrooms and doorways is not shown. Trace this frame onto a separate sheet of paper. Use a pencil and press lightly. Leave room for a legend. Show the four cardinal points.

The smaller drawing below is a map or **floor plan** of the same school showing the rooms. It includes the location of all the hallways, walls and doorways. Create a legend for these features and add it to your drawing. When would you use a floor plan of a building?

Fit the frame you have drawn to the floor plan and keep it fitted as you draw. You are now ready to add the rooms and doorways. Think about the best way to complete your task; that is, plan your work. Where should you start? The rooms and doorways in your finished drawing must be in the same pattern as the ones in the floor plan. The shape and direction of the hallways and outside walls can help you draw the rooms accurately.

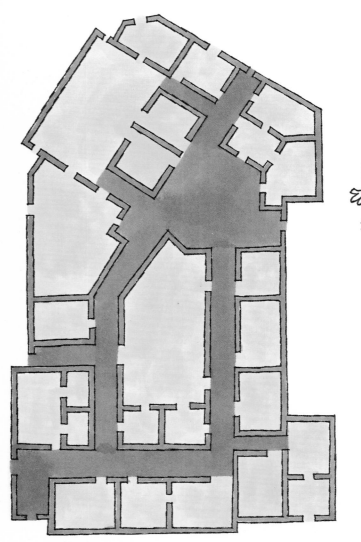

0  3  6  9  12  15  18  21  24  27  30 m

*1 cm represents 3 m*

Check your finished work very carefully from all sides. Let someone else look at it. When you are satisfied, go over the lines with a pen or heavy pencil.

Use the line scale below the frame and a ruler to answer the following questions:

- How wide are the main halls in real life?
- How long is the longest north/south hall?
- What is the greatest east/west distance between the outside walls?

On pages 14 and 15 you learned how to use a grid to locate places and give directions. Draw a grid on your floor plan. Work with a partner to see if he or she can find you in the school when given a grid reference.

# Camp Bug-a-View

**View 1**

Welcome to summer camp! Here are two different views of Camp Bug-a-View. Where would you be to see each of these views?

Cover up View 2. Write a brief description of what you can see in View 1.

Uncover View 2 and compare it to View 1. What different comments might you have made about the things you saw in View 1 (the view from the side) now that you have had the advantage of seeing the camp from above (View 2).

Make a list of the things you can see in the view from above that you cannot see in the view from the side. Also, what objects are you not able to see from above that you could see from the side view?

What conclusions can you make about the shape of objects when viewed from different angles? In your opinion, what are the advantages of a view of places from above?

Who would find this map of Camp Bug-a-View useful?

**View 2**

# Traffic Helicopter

You are visiting a busy city area in the early morning. You will see the area from three points of view: from the street level, from a rooftop, and from a traffic helicopter.

Make a list of everything you can see at the street level view of the city.

What additional things can you see from the rooftop view?

You are now in a traffic helicopter. You are filling in for the radio traffic reporter and must provide information that will help motorists travelling to work.

Study the streets and traffic flow very carefully. Prepare a one-minute report making note of construction sites, accidents, and any other problems that you can see which would be of interest to motorists. Be prepared to read your report to your radio listeners.

**Street level view**

**Rooftop view**

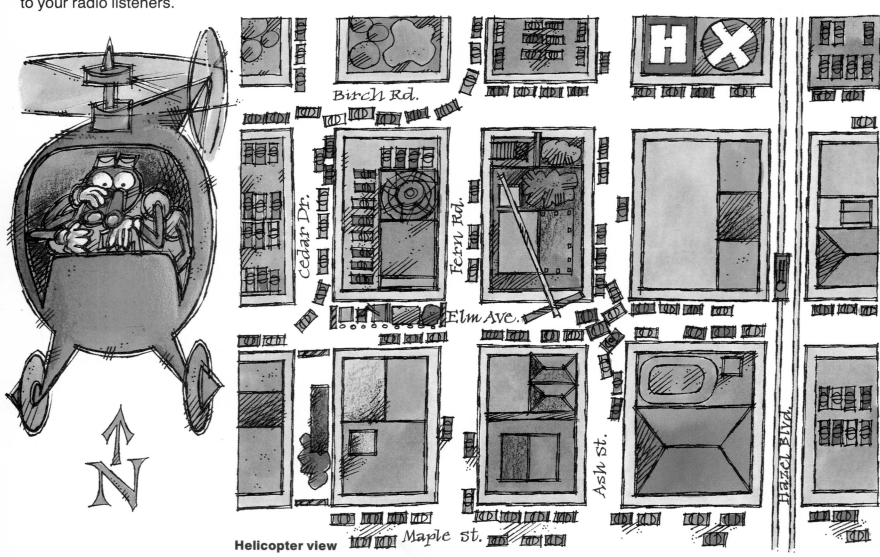

**Helicopter view**

# Hisses, Barks, and Squeaks

You have been asked to plan how the space in a pet store will be used. Should some pets be kept away from each other? Why?

Trace the shape of the containers shown for the different pets. Cut out each shape. Create a way of identifying each one.

Make a copy of the frame of the store with the doorway and sales counter as shown.

Kittens

Parrot

Snake

Mynah bird

Lizard

Hamsters

Tropical fish

Tarantula

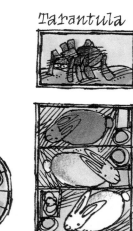

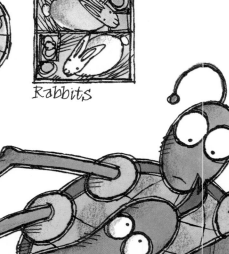

Puppies

Budgies

Rabbits

White mice

Plan your pet store. Try more than one arrangement of containers within the frame. Will the pets be happy beside each other?

Once you are satisfied, trace around each shape and remove the cutouts. Identify each pet location on your plan. Congratulations! You have drawn a map of the pet store.

Compare your map to someone else's map.

# Room Jumble

Why would somebody have difficulty living in this apartment? Make a list of some of the problems that you would have if you lived here.

How is your bedroom at home organized? Is the way you organize your living space important? Why?

Draw a frame of the apartment in the picture showing only the walls, windows, and doorways. Plan a new location for the important objects in each room so that the space is used in a way that would be best for you.

Fixed objects such as the sink and toilet in the bathroom cannot be moved. Once you are satisfied with your plan, add these objects to your frame to create a map of the apartment.

In planning the use of space in each room, what items did you have to consider first? Work with another person to develop a set of rules which would help others to organize objects in a living space.

# Hide and Seek

Choose a partner to play *Hide and Seek*. The purpose of this game is to practice using location words to help you to find a specific place.

Imagine that you are tiny enough to live in this miniature village. Your partner is to select a building in which to hide. You are to try to find the building in which your partner is hiding by asking no more than *seven* questions. How can you plan your questions so that you get close to the hiding place as quickly as possible? Your choice of location words will be important to your success.

Your partner may only answer "yes" or "no" to your questions. If you do not discover the hiding place in seven questions, your partner may hide again in a different location. Take turns hiding.

Now think of a real place in the room you are in. Can your partner guess the place you are thinking of by asking questions using location words?

# Small Is Big

Here is an activity to give you more practice at finding the real-life size of objects using a line scale with drawings which are smaller.

You already know what a line scale is and how to use it. The word **scale** may be used by itself. For example, the scale of all the objects shown here is *smaller* than real life. They had to be drawn that way in order to fit them on the page. Scale is the size of something compared to its real-life size. A scale may also be bigger than real life.

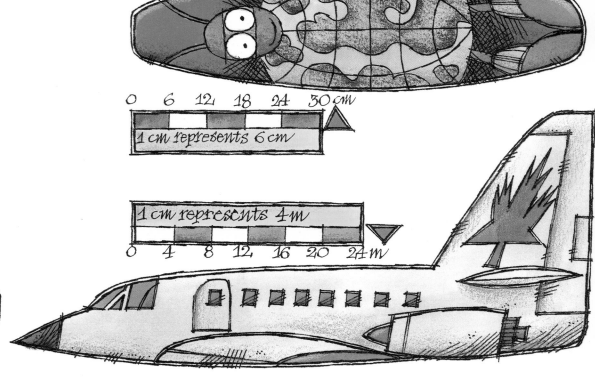

0   6   12   18   24   30 cm

1 cm represents 6 cm

1 cm represents 4 m

0   4   8   12   16   20   24 m

0   10   20   30   40 cm

1 cm represents 10 cm

0   25   50   75   100   125   150   175   200 cm

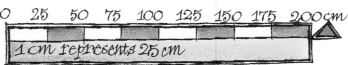

1 cm represents 25 cm

0   3   6   9   cm

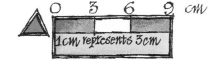

1 cm represents 3 cm

Look at each drawing. What problems would you have trying to compare scales if you had never seen these objects before and there were no line scales?

Use the line scale for each object to find out its real-life length. Use an organizer to record your measurements.

Any object may be drawn or made smaller than its real-life size. It can be a little smaller or a lot smaller. The closer an object is to its real-life size, the *larger* the scale. The farther away an object is from its real-life size, the *smaller* the scale.

What object on this page is nearest to its real-life size? This object has the *largest* scale compared to the other objects.

What object is farthest away from real-life size? This object has the *smallest* scale compared to the other objects.

# Looking Down From a Blimp

Here is another look at **large scale** and **small scale**.

Imagine that you are in a blimp over a baseball stadium. Everything in the picture of the stadium looks a lot smaller than real-life size. The artist has used a small scale to show you as much as possible using only a part of this page.

List some of the things you can see. Can you describe in detail what the baseball players are wearing? What is meant by "detail"?

The picture on the left is what Globug sees using binoculars. It shows the action at first base. The players look closer to real-life size than those in the view from the blimp. The artist has used a large scale. We can now see the players' uniforms in detail.

List in detail what the players are wearing.

What conclusions can you make about things drawn or made using a large scale compared to a small scale?

What kinds of maps should be drawn using a large scale?

# Cardinal Park

Cardinal Park is a very busy place on weekends. There is activity going on in all directions.

Imagine you are standing at the fountain beside Globug. Look in the direction of each of the four cardinal points. For each direction name two things that you can see.

There are many things to see if you look in other directions. If you look at the compass below you will discover there are points between the cardinal points. These are called **intercardinal points**. They are *northwest, northeast, southwest,* and *southeast,* or NW, NE, SW, and SE.

Look in the direction of each of the four intercardinal points. For each direction, name one thing that you can see.

Use your imagination and try the following game with a partner. Find a place in the park to relax. Use cardinal and intercardinal points to give the direction of three things that you can see from where you are. Can your partner find where you are relaxing?

# Runway Approach

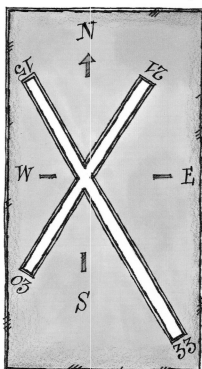

This is a photograph of Buttonville Airport taken from an airplane. What do we call this view?

There are four numbered runways on which airplanes can land. How would you describe the direction of each runway using intercardinal points? Use the small runway drawing to help you with the answers.

How do you think the numbers on the runways are used?

Pilots like to land and take off "into the wind."

This means that when airplanes are using the runways, the wind should be blowing towards the front of the planes, rather than the back.

You are now working in the air traffic control tower at Buttonville. One of your jobs is to tell pilots about wind direction and what runways to use. Cardinal or intercardinal points are used to name wind direction. For example, there are west winds, north winds, and southwest winds. The name of the wind always tells you the direction *from* which it is blowing. If you look to the west when a west wind is blowing, you will feel it on your face.

In what direction does a southwest wind blow?

Copy the organizer. The left column has a list of five different winds. The middle column is for the direction in which each wind blows. The right column is for the runway number that pilots should use so that they land into the wind. The first one has been done for you. For cardinal-point winds there will be two possible runways.

| wind | wind blows towards | use runway number |
|------|--------------------|--------------------|
| south northwest southeast northeast north | north | 15 or 21 |

Before you leave this page, spend some time studying the photograph. Look at all the different shapes. How many different things can you see? Create symbols for each of the main features that you would put on a map of this photograph.

# The World of Orienteering

**Orienteering** is a sport and recreational activity which requires the use of a map to find your way from place to place.

You are to plan a three-hour orienteering hike with this map. Start and finish at the building beside the parking lot.

Study the legend very carefully. Look at the way colors are used. The colors shown here, which represent water, marsh, open area, and forest, are the colors used on orienteering maps all over the world.

Decide which places you would like to visit and then plan a route that will allow you to visit these places in three hours.

How far do you think you can hike in 30 min? Most people can walk from 3 km to 4 km in an hour. Use this as a guide in estimating how long it will take you to travel from place to place. Use the line scale to obtain the approximate distance.

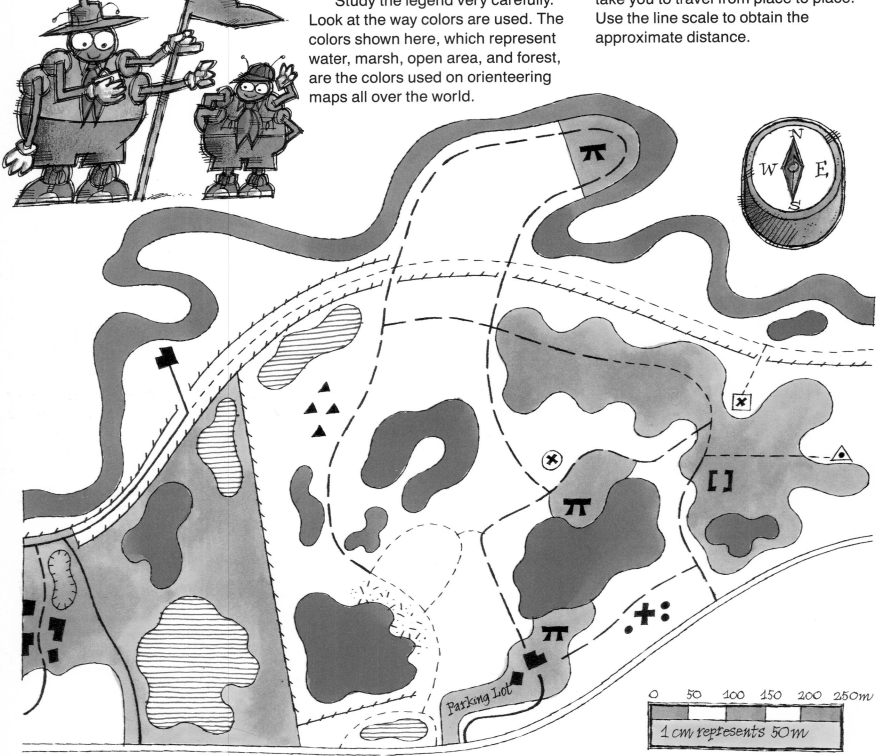

0    50    100    150    200    250m

1 cm represents 50m

Parking Lot

| | | | |
|---|---|---|---|
| ═══ highway | ✚ pile of stones | ⊗ ant hill |
| ─── gravel road | • boulder | ▲▲ bat caves |
| ‒ ‒ dirt road | water | ☒ deer station |
| ---- trail | marsh | fossils |
| ⊥⊥ fence | open area | △ lookout |
| buildings | forest | ⊓⊓ picnic area |
| [ ] ruin | gravel pit | |

Write a brief description of the hike you have planned. Make reference to the directions in which you will travel by using cardinal and intercardinal points. Describe the different types of scenery you will pass and the places you will visit.

# Highs and Lows

Make a list of all the colors used in the picture above. What color has been used to show lowlands? Look at the hills. What three colors have been used to show different heights?

The four colors used in this way are symbols for land heights.

The map and the picture above are of the same place. Look at the hills on the map. Can you imagine their shape from the side without looking at the picture?

The color for water is usually blue. Why? Why do you think dark green is often used for lowlands?

The same colors for land heights will be used on many of the maps later in this book.

Draw a map of the picture below. Make a legend. Use boxes with the same four colors that are used on this page to show land heights. Dark green will be called *lowlands*. What will you call the other three colors?

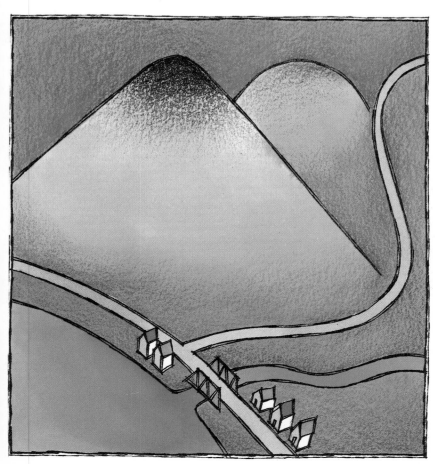

Your turn!

# Mall Madness

You have had some practice using a grid to locate places on maps. Now you will learn some other ways that help people to find places they want to visit.

You are going to visit West Edmonton Mall in Edmonton, Alberta. Look at the map of the roads around the mall. What can you say about the road numbers from east to west and south to north? How would that help people find their way to the mall?

West Edmonton Mall is shown in the shaded area. Describe its location using road names. How do the words "avenue" and "street" help with direction?

The mall is said to be the size of 115 football fields. Use the line scale to measure its approximate length and width in metres.

When you visit the mall you can obtain a guide brochure. It has lists of all the stores and maps of the main and second floor. The maps you see on these two pages are similar to the ones in the guide. What do you call these kinds of maps?

Every store in the mall has a number. You can see these numbers on each of the floor plans. Look at the numbers used for the main floor and the second floor. How do the store numbers help people find their way?

The letters in black boxes on each floor show "areas." In what areas on the second floor are The Bay, Woodward's, and Canadian Tire?

Look at the area letters for both floors. How have they been organized to help you find your way?

You are going to visit some clothing stores on the second floor. To find each store you will use its area letter and number from a list in the mall shopping guide shown below. How quickly can you find each store?

| | |
|---|---|
| Coconut Joe | R2131 |
| Roots | U2414 |
| T'Shirts and Things | W2584 |
| Sears | Z2950 |
| Just Coats | Q2045 |
| Club Monaco | T2359 |
| Thrifty's | V2564 |
| Zellers | S2185 |

If you lose something in the mall you can try the Lost and Found at Y2872.

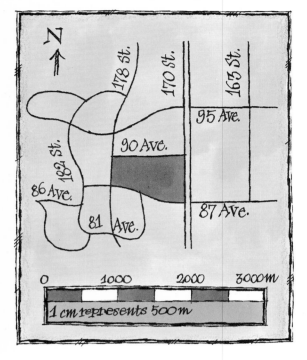

## SECOND FLOOR

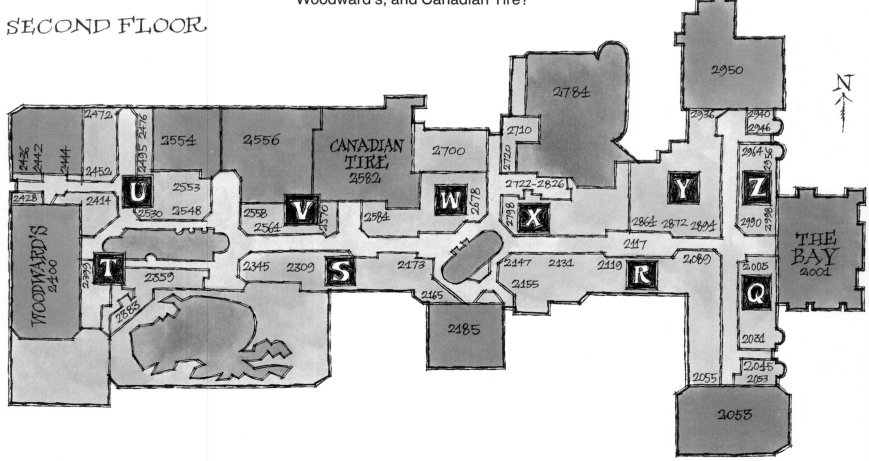

# MAIN FLOOR

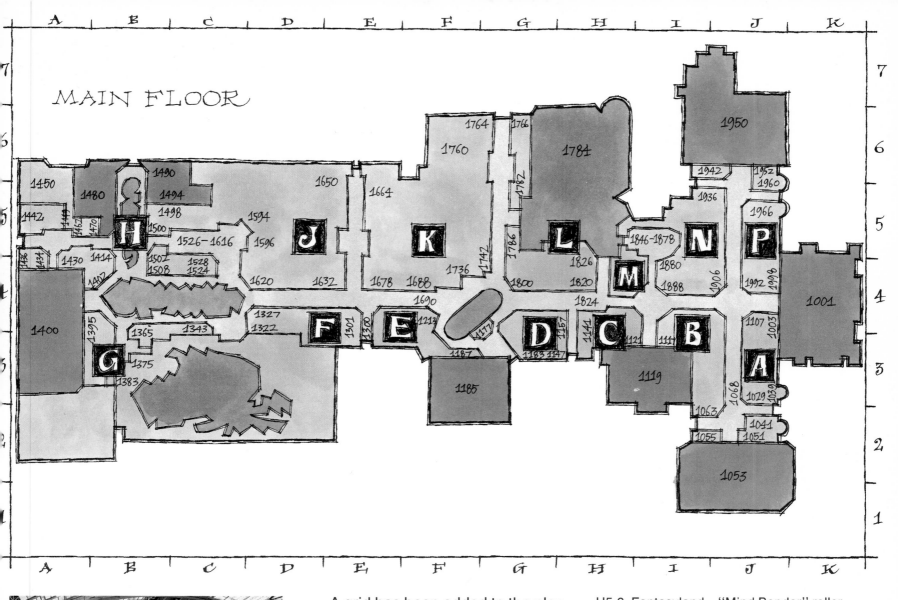

A grid has been added to the plan of the main floor. You are going to spend a day at the mall and have some fun. Look at the list of places to see and things to do. Each place has a grid reference for the area in which it can be found. Copy the organizer and use it to plan your activities for the morning and the afternoon. What things should you consider in planning your day?

| grid reference | morning activity | grid reference | afternoon activity |
| --- | --- | --- | --- |
| | | | |

| | |
| --- | --- |
| H5,6 | Fantasyland—"Mind Bender" roller coaster, animal petting zoo |
| C4 | Deep Sea Adventure—submarine rides and dolphins |
| D4 | Computers |
| G5 | Video Games |
| I5 | Gourmet World—pizza, tacos, seafood, deli, Chinese and Japanese food |
| D5 | Movie Theatres |
| C4 | Sea Life Caverns—penguins, seals, sharks |
| F4 | Ice Palace—figure skaters, professional hockey practice |
| B5 | Pebble Beach Golf Course—18-hole miniature golf course |
| E4 | Ice Cream |
| I4 | Toys |
| G5 | McDonald's |
| C4 | Santa Maria—life-size model of Columbus' sailing ship |
| B5 | Pet Store |
| C3 | Waterpark—"Raging Rapids" inner tube ride, "Big Thunder" wave |
| B3 | Records and Tapes |

When you have finished, compare your planned day with someone else's plan. Which of the two ways for finding places in the mall did you like better? Why?

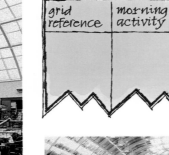

# Mapping the Front of the School

Here is a view of the front of Globug's school as seen from the roof. You are going to draw a map of this area.

Make an inventory of all the things that you want on your map. Remember, choose features that can be seen from above and seldom or never change location.

Your next step is to draw a symbol to represent each feature. If you have forgotten the rules for creating symbols, look back at page 16.

Below you will see that Globug has already started to draw. Look at the symbol used for the school. Is it the same as yours? Name the other symbol in the legend. How did you make the symbols for sidewalk, path, and driveway look different?

Make a copy of Globug's frame which is shown below. Add your legend. Keep the frame fitted as you work. It is helpful to add the driveway and parking lot next. Why? Drawing the large features first and adding the small features last is good planning. Remember to press lightly with your pencil and keep the map fitted at all times.

When you have finished, check that the size and spacing of your symbols match the features in the picture. It helps if you look at your drawing from different places. For example, from the flag pole check to see if the sign, tree, and lights are in the correct space. Move to one end of the bicycle rack and look at other places on your map. Do they match the picture? If everything seems to line up correctly then redraw the lines in dark pencil.

Do you think you could draw a map of the front of your school? List the steps you would follow.

LEGEND
school

# Mapping the Whole Schoolyard

By getting higher and changing location, Globug is able to see the whole schoolyard. Mapping this area is more challenging than doing the front of the school. List some reasons why.

Begin by preparing a legend. Follow the same plan as you did when mapping other areas.

You will have to create a frame. Will it be a square or a rectangle? What features from your legend will you use as the sides of the frame? What large feature can you include in the frame to help you find the correct location of other features as you draw them? Remember to leave room on your paper for the legend.

If you included the school in the frame you made a good choice. Is it in the correct space? Look at the picture. Which half of the schoolyard is it in? How would you describe its location between the fences on each side? The school in your drawing should occupy the same amount of space, compared to other features, as the school in the picture.

Remember to keep the frame fitted when you draw. Work from large feature to small until everything in your legend has been added.

Check your map for accuracy. Fit it to the picture. With your finger, move to different locations on the map. Do your symbols line up in the same way as their features in the picture? If some of your symbols look crowded then they may be too large. Let another person look at your map. It should be easy for anyone to understand without asking questions.

What steps would you follow to make a map of your schoolyard?

# Mapping Down the Street

Globug has just started a balloon ride over the neighborhood around the school. Mapping down the street is your next challenge. That should be no problem because you have a step-by-step plan for mapping and lots of experience.

Prepare your legend. On a sheet of paper in the upper left-hand corner draw the cardinal points. Add your legend to the bottom of the sheet.

You are ready to draw your frame. It will look different from others you have prepared. The street with a feature at each end will be the frame. Call it a **line frame**. The intersection should be at the top of your sheet and run in the same direction as the one in the picture. In what directions does the street with the bend run? Look at page 26 if you need some help. Add the fence to complete your frame.

You are now ready to add other features, from large to small. Keep your frame fitted. The bend in the road is a good reference for helping you to find the correct space for the bridge and the house. Is the house nearer to the bend or to the fence? The symbol for house on your map should be spaced the same way. One of the street lights is at the bend in the road. That's an easy one to add. Complete your map and compare it to the picture before you redraw the lines with a dark pencil.

Describe how you would map a sidewalk or road near you.

# Mapping a Trip

Tomorrow you will be travelling by bus to visit a zoo.

You are to draw a map from a written description of the route you will take to the zoo. Here is the description.

## Bus Trip to the Zoo

The bus will travel to a large highway about 1 km north of the school. We will stay on this highway, which runs westwards, for about 20 km. After travelling 1 km on the highway, we will see a golf course on the south side of the road. Then 5 km later we will stop to visit an old windmill in the village of Grafton. The River Grafton runs north to south through the village. The village of Oakridge is 6 km beyond Grafton. Here we will see the famous giant oak tree that is said to be hundreds of years old. You have been to Oakridge to play baseball in the diamond to the north of the village. We will travel a further 7 km to a favorite stop for travellers. On the south side of the highway is a park with a pond and picnic area. On the opposite side is a historic monument dedicated to the first settlers of this area. Near the end of the highway we will turn north on to a side road and travel 2 km to the zoo. Just east of the zoo is one of the largest ice cream stores you have ever seen. I wonder if . . . .

To make a map of the route, first prepare the legend. Remember to include in your legend all the features you will show on your map.

Add the cardinal points, making sure that north is pointing to the top of your page.

Draw a line scale 7 cm long using 1 cm to represent each kilometre of real-life or **actual** distance.

You are now ready to begin drawing your map. Use the description of the trip to the zoo to help you draw the line frame. How long is the highway on your map? What feature will you draw at each end of the highway? Find the other features in the description and add them to your map.

Which will be easier to follow as you travel to the zoo—your map or the written description? Why?

# Mapping a Large Area

Your task is to make a map of Canada's smallest province, Prince Edward Island. How large is the island? Use the line scale to discover its approximate length and width.

Make a list of all the important features you will want to show on the map and create symbols for them.

The main feature is the coastline. Draw or trace an outline to represent the island.

Select another important feature, such as the Trans-Canada Highway or the railway line, and draw the symbol on the map. Use the outline of the coast to help you place the features accurately.

Add the symbols for other features to complete the map.

Indicate the cardinal and intercardinal points.

Add a grid so that features can be referenced. Refer to page 14 if you need help.

Well done! You have drawn a map of a whole province.

Write three questions which could be answered by using your finished map. For example: In which direction would you travel if you went from Charlottetown to Kensington? What is the grid reference for Elmira? Have someone answer your questions.

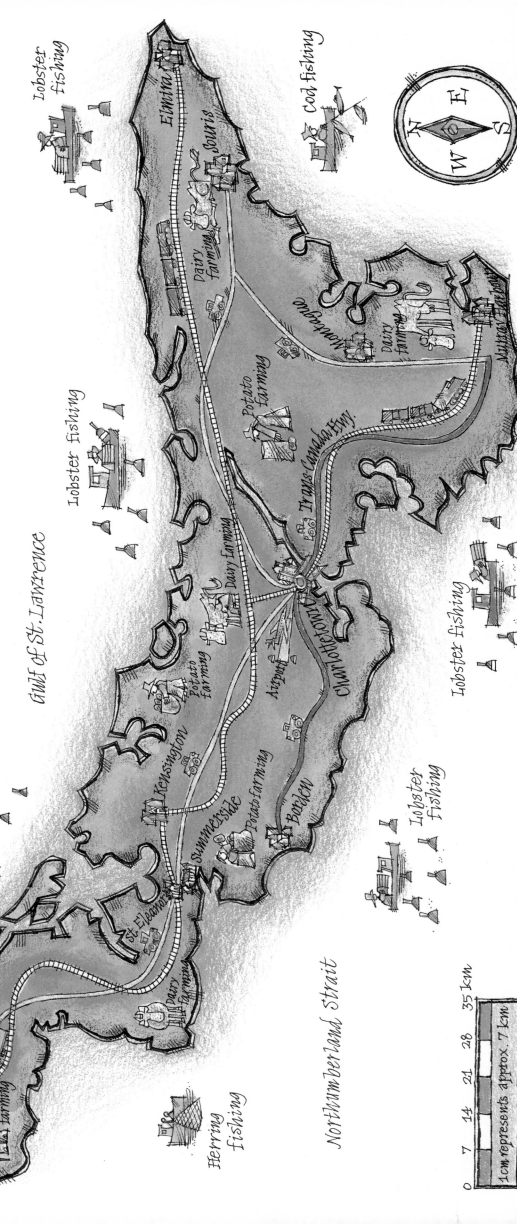

# O Canada!

This picture of Canada is unusual. It is made up of electronic signals beamed to computers from a satellite orbiting in space. Its color is different too. The infra-red signals show all vegetation as red. The darker the red, the healthier the vegetation. The white areas show either places where signals did not register or places with some snow cover. To make identification of certain areas easier, some boundaries have been added to this picture.

Locate the darker area of healthy coniferous forest that covers much of Canada. Locate the lighter red areas. These indicate farming areas. Why do you think these areas appear as a lighter red?

What would city areas look like? Can you see any?

Trace the outline of France. How many times does it fit into the area of Canada shown.

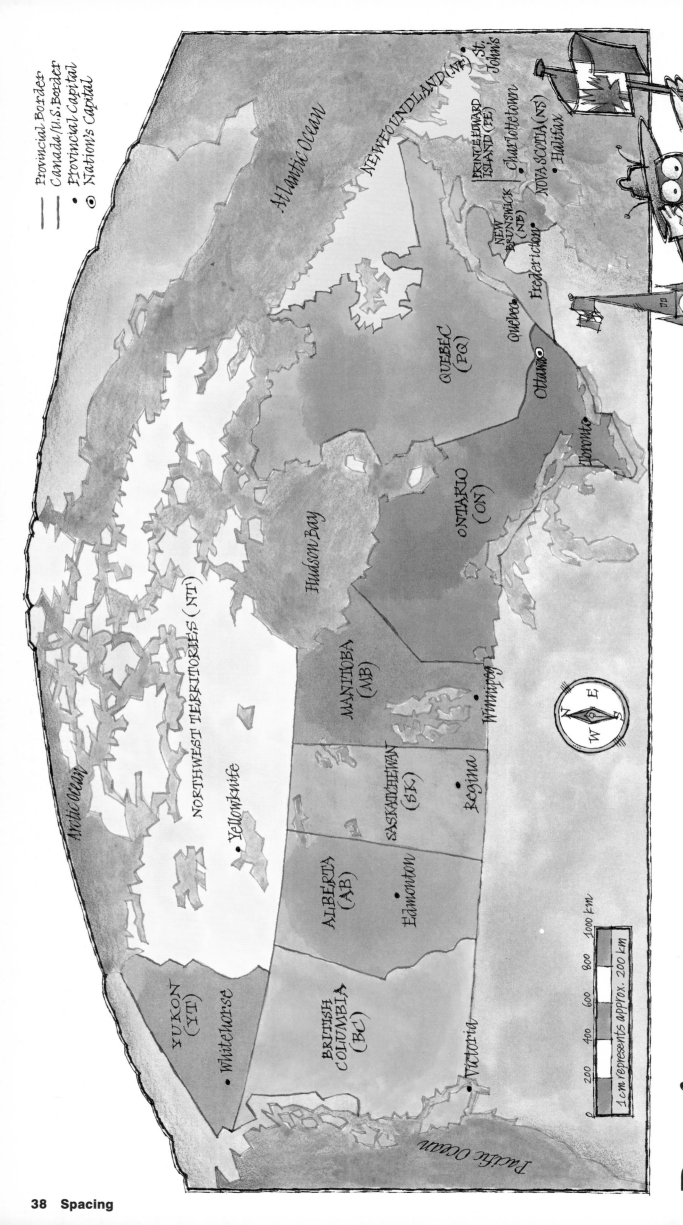

# Provinces and Territories

Study this map of Canada and list the provinces and Territories in order of approximate size from the smallest to the largest.

You have been asked to visit all the provincial and Territorial capital cities from Newfoundland to British Columbia. List the cities in the order in which you would visit them.

Use the line scale to find out the approximate distance you would travel between each city and the total distance you would travel on your trip.

# Free Range Landforms

Canada contains great mountain ranges, rolling plains, and fertile lowlands. These make up some of the landform regions that form this vast country. Few other countries in the world have the variety of landforms that Canada contains.

Copy the organizer and complete the information for each province and Territory. An example has been provided.

| province/territory | landform |
|---|---|
| Saskatchewan | interior plains with some Canadian Shield in north |

What are the three mountain passes that allow travel between British Columbia and Alberta?

Where could you go if you were to go mountaineering? Find each of the features mentioned in the *Scuttlebug*. Give the grid references for each feature.

## SCUTTLEBUG

**Longest river:**
Mackenzie River—4241 km
**Highest mountain:**
Mt. Logan, YT—5951 m
**Largest island:**
Baffin Island, NT—507 450 km²
**Largest lake:**
Great Bear, NT—31 328 km²

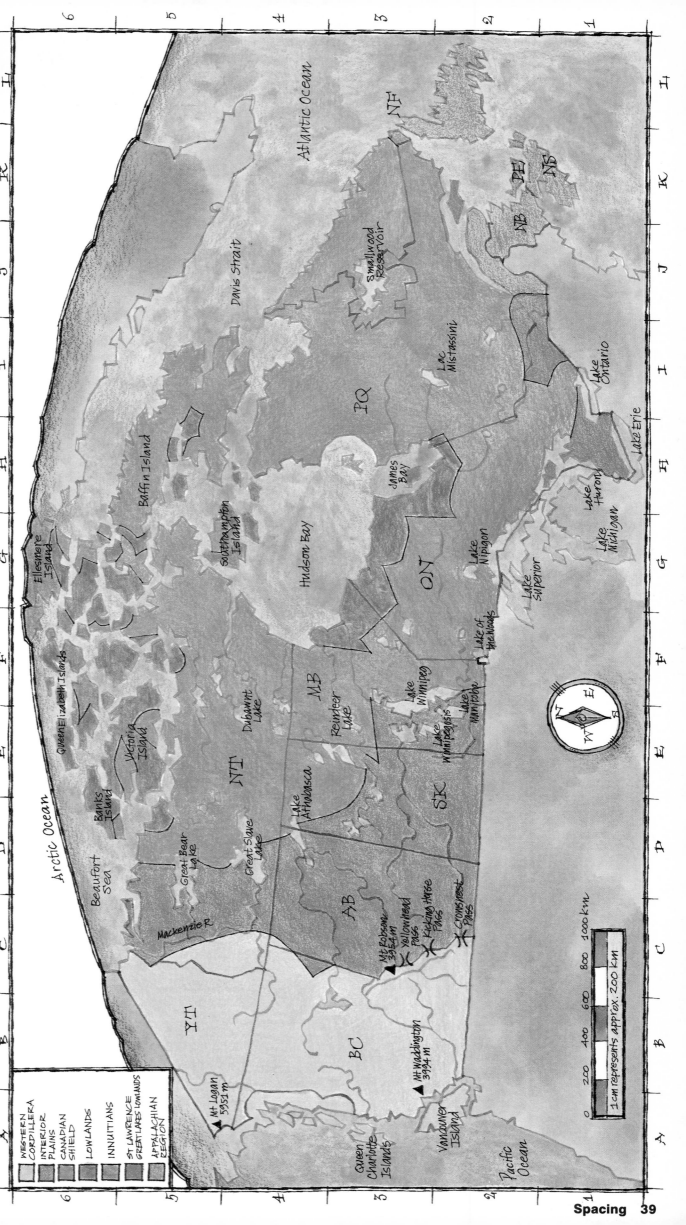

Legend:
- WESTERN CORDILLERA
- INTERIOR PLAINS
- CANADIAN SHIELD
- LOWLANDS
- INNUITIANS
- ST LAWRENCE GREAT LAKES LOWLANDS
- APPALACHIAN REGION

1 cm represents approx. 200 km

# Seasons in the Sun

As Canada is such a large country, it has a number of different climates.

Copy and complete the organizer to describe the summer and winter climate for each of the six places shown on the map. An example is provided.

| Location | Temperature | | Precipitation |
|---|---|---|---|
| | summer | winter | |
| Halifax | 15 to 20°C mild-warm | -10 to 0°C very cold | 1000 - 2000 mm |

*January Temperature*

*July Temperature*

Select one location that you would like to visit both in January and July. Write down a list of the clothing you think you would need for each occasion.

*Precipitation*

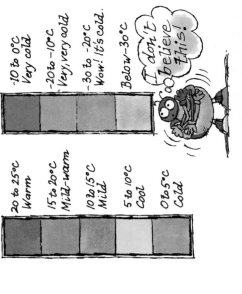

| | |
|---|---|
| 20 to 25°C Warm | -10 to 0°C Very cold |
| 15 to 20°C Mild-warm | -20 to -10°C Very, very cold |
| 10 to 15°C Mild | -30 to -20°C Wow! It's cold. |
| 5 to 10°C Cool | Below -30°C |
| 0 to 5°C Cold | |

more than 2000 mm
1000 - 2000 mm
600 - 1000 mm
400 - 600 mm
200 - 400 mm
less than 200 mm

SCUTTLEBUG

**Highest temperature:** 45°C, Midale and Yellow Grass, SK—July 5, 1937
**Lowest temperature:** -63°C, Snag, YT—February 3, 1947
**Most precipitation in one year:** 812 cm, Henderson Lake, BC—1931
**Most snowfall in one day:** 118 cm, Lakelse Lake, BC—January 17, 1974
**Strongest wind:** 203 km/h, Cape-Hopes-Advance, PQ—November 18, 1931

# Vegging Out

You are a bush pilot flying north. The dotted line on the map traces your route. Draw a line to represent the distance travelled by the plane. Divide the line into the vegetation areas you will see along the way. Be sure to keep the distances of the vegetation areas the same as on the map.

In which vegetation areas are Canada's principal cities located?

What can you conclude about the location of the principal cities and the surrounding vegetation?

- tundra and ice cap
- northern coniferous forest
- mountain coniferous forest
- grazing land
- irrigated land
- farmland
- marsh
- deciduous and mixed forest
- ▲▲▲ tree line

## SCUTTLEBUG

Total forested area: 4 365 000 km$^2$
Coniferous: 80%
Deciduous: 20%

**Most common trees**

| | | |
|---|---|---|
| Spruce: 31% | Hemlock: 6% | Maple: 3% |
| Pine: 16% | Birch 5% | Others: 7% |
| Fir: 14% | Cedar: 4% | |
| Poplar: 11% | Douglas Fir: 3% | |

1% of all Canada's trees are burned accidentally each year!

YT
• Whitehorse

BC
• Vancouver

NT
• Yellowknife

AB
• Edmonton
• Calgary

SK
• Regina

MB
• Winnipeg

ON
Ottawa
• Toronto
Hamilton •
• St. Catharines/Niagara

PQ
Quebec •
• Montreal

NF
• St. John's

NB
Saint John •

PE • Charlottetown

NS
• Halifax

0  200  400  600  800  1000 km
1 cm represents approx. 200 km

N
E
W
S

# Canada Grows Up

European settlement in this vast land we call Canada followed the arrival of the early explorers. In the 1700s colonies were founded by Britain and France. These colonies eventually were divided into the provinces and Territories to form the country that we see today. Changes came gradually. On pages 42 and 43 are five maps which show the shape and size of Canada at important dates in its history.

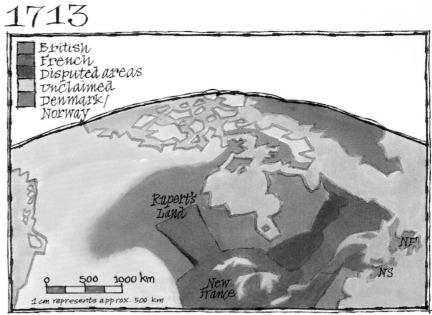

**1713**

Legend:
British
French
Disputed areas
Unclaimed
Denmark/Norway

Rupert's Land
New France
NF
NS

0    500    1000 km
1 cm represents approx. 500 km

**Prior to the establishment of colonies in the 1700s, there were many visits by Europeans looking for furs and fish.**

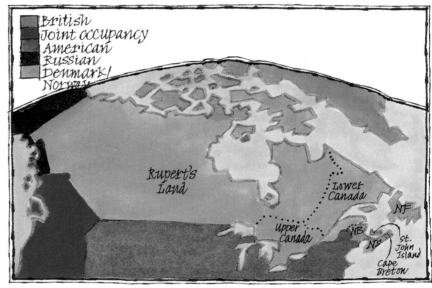

**1784**

Legend:
British
Joint occupancy
American
Russian
Denmark/Norway

Rupert's Land
Lower Canada
Upper Canada
NF
NB
NS
St. John Island
Cape Breton

**The Constitutional Act of 1791 divided Canada into two parts. What were they?**

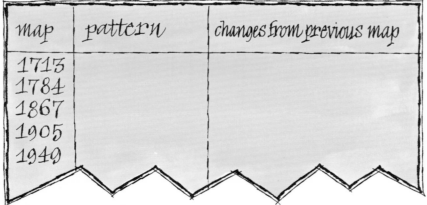

| map | pattern | changes from previous map |
|-----|---------|---------------------------|
| 1713 | | |
| 1784 | | |
| 1867 | | |
| 1905 | | |
| 1949 | | |

Use a copy of the organizer to compare the maps. What are the changes which you can identify from map to map?

Research to find out what you can about one of the following explorers: Cabot, Frobisher, Davis, Hudson, Baffin, Franklin, Champlain, Mackenzie, Thompson, Fraser.

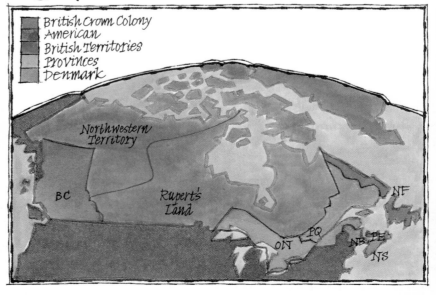

**1867**

Legend:
British Crown Colony
American
British Territories
Provinces
Denmark

Northwestern Territory
BC
Rupert's Land
NF
ON
PQ
NB
PE
NS

**In 1867 the Dominion of Canada was formed. What were the founding provinces?**

# 1905

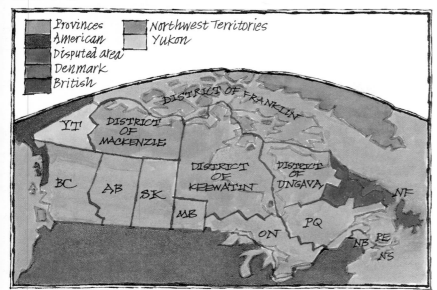

Legend:
- Provinces
- American
- Disputed area
- Denmark
- British
- Northwest Territories
- Yukon

**Between 1867 and 1905, new provinces were added. What were they?**

Use the organizer to compare the lifestyle of the European settlers in 1867 with our lifestyle today. Refer to the illustration below and also visit a resource centre to help you in your research.

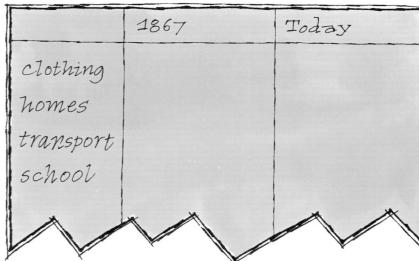

|          | 1867 | Today |
|----------|------|-------|
| clothing |      |       |
| homes    |      |       |
| transport|      |       |
| school   |      |       |

# 1949

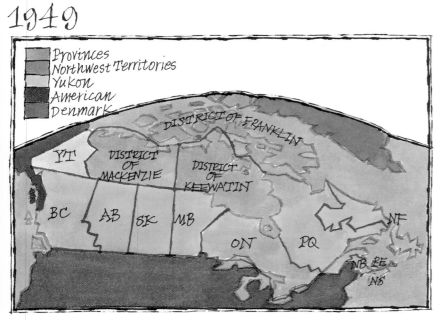

Legend:
- Provinces
- Northwest Territories
- Yukon
- American
- Denmark

**The Canada that we see today was completed with the addition of the tenth province. Which province was the last to join Canada?**

St. Lawrence riverboat

MONTREAL

steam locomotive

oil lamp

fuel saver stove

butter churn

chalkboard

magic lantern

school desk

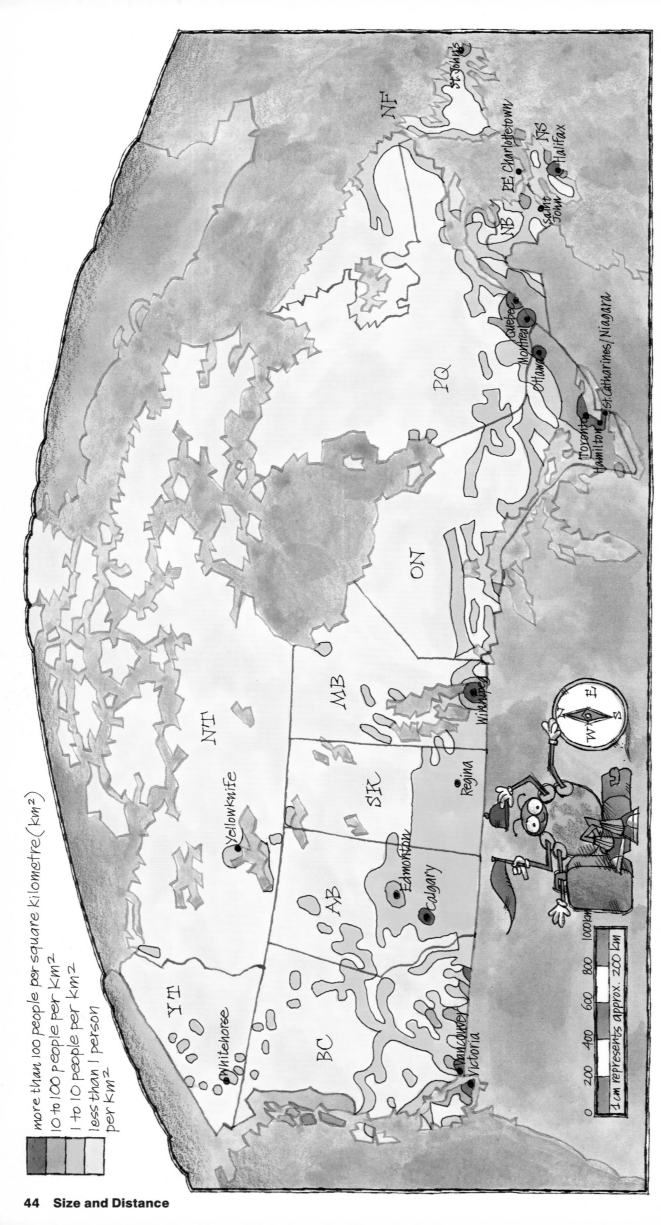

more than 100 people per square kilometre (km²)

10 to 100 people per km²

1 to 10 people per km²

less than 1 person per km²

1 cm represents approx. 200 km

0   200   400   600   800   1000 km

SCUTTLEBUG

**Top Ten Metropolitan Areas**

| | |
|---|---|
| Toronto, ON | 3 427 000 |
| Montreal, PQ | 2 921 000 |
| Vancouver, BC | 1 380 000 |
| Ottawa-Hull, PQ | 819 000 |
| Edmonton, AB | 785 000 |
| Calgary, AB | 671 000 |
| Winnipeg, MB | 625 000 |
| Quebec, PQ | 603 000 |
| Hamilton, ON | 557 000 |
| St. Catharines/Niagara, ON | 343 000 |

FACT! Nearly one in every three Canadians lives in Ontario. Highest city in Canada: Rossland, BC (1056 m)

# Where People Live

How many of Canada's principal cities are within 400 km of the border with the United States and how many are further away? Use the line scale to assist you. Why do you think so many people live close to the border?

If you draw a line between Victoria, British Columbia, and St. John's, Newfoundland, which provincial boundary is nearest to the centre of that line? How many principal cities are to the east of that central boundary? How many are there to the west of that central boundary? What can you conclude about the distribution of Canada's principal cities in relation to the central provincial boundary and an imaginary line running 400 km north of the United States border?

Approximately how far would you have to travel from your home to a convention in Canada's largest city?

# A Huge Country

Canada is so large that it is divided into different time zones. How many different time zones are there in Canada and what are they called?

What other country has time zones similar to Canada's?

When Globug is starting school at 09:00 in Vancouver, British Columbia, what time is it in Ottawa, Ontario; Halifax, Nova Scotia; Calgary, Alberta?

If you wanted to watch a special presentation that was being televised live from Edmonton at noon, mountain time, what time would you have to switch on your television set?

Use the line scale to find the approximate coast-to-coast distance using the Trans-Canada Highway.

Complete the organizer below by listing some of the advantages (pluses), disadvantages (minuses), and interesting things about the large size of Canada.

| pluses | minuses | interesting |
|--------|---------|-------------|
|        |         |             |
|        |         |             |

1 cm represents approx. 200 km

0   200   400   600   800   1000 km

# Roll River Roll

You have been asked to plan a trip down the Mackenzie River starting at Yellowknife, Northwest Territories.

In which direction does the river flow? Which communities will you pass along the route?

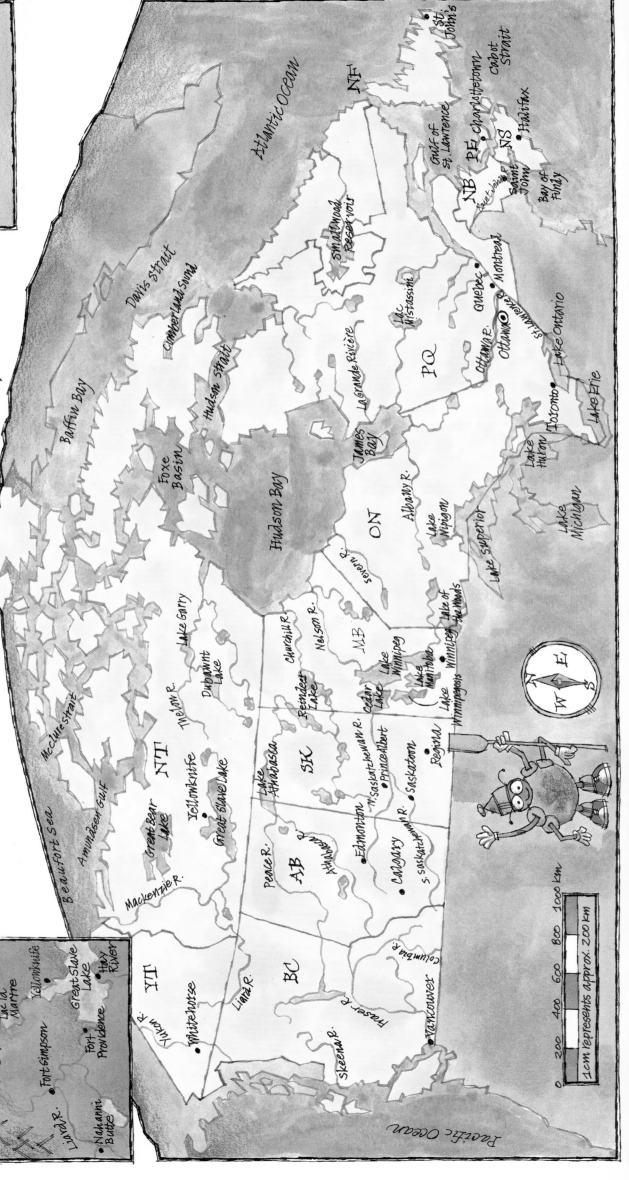

Complete a copy of the organizer below which looks at important rivers in Canada. On pages 42 and 43 you investigated early European explorers. Name the explorers who have had rivers named after them. In which provinces are these rivers located?

| river | where it starts (source) | where it ends (mouth) | direction of flow | towns and cities |
|---|---|---|---|---|
| South Saskatchewan | Rocky Mountains | Cedar Lake | easterly | Saskatoon |

SCUTTLEBUG

**Largest Rivers in Canada**
1. Mackenzie River .......... 4 241 km
2. Yukon River .............. 3 185 km
3. St. Lawrence River ....... 3 058 km
4. Nelson River ............. 2 557 km
5. Columbia River ........... 2 000 km

**Longest Rivers in the World**
1. Nile, Africa ................. 6 695 km
2. Amazon, South America ... 6 437 km
3. Chang Jiang, Asia .......... 6 380 km
4. Mississippi-Missouri, USA . 5 971 km
5. Ob-Irtysh, Asia ............ 5 410 km

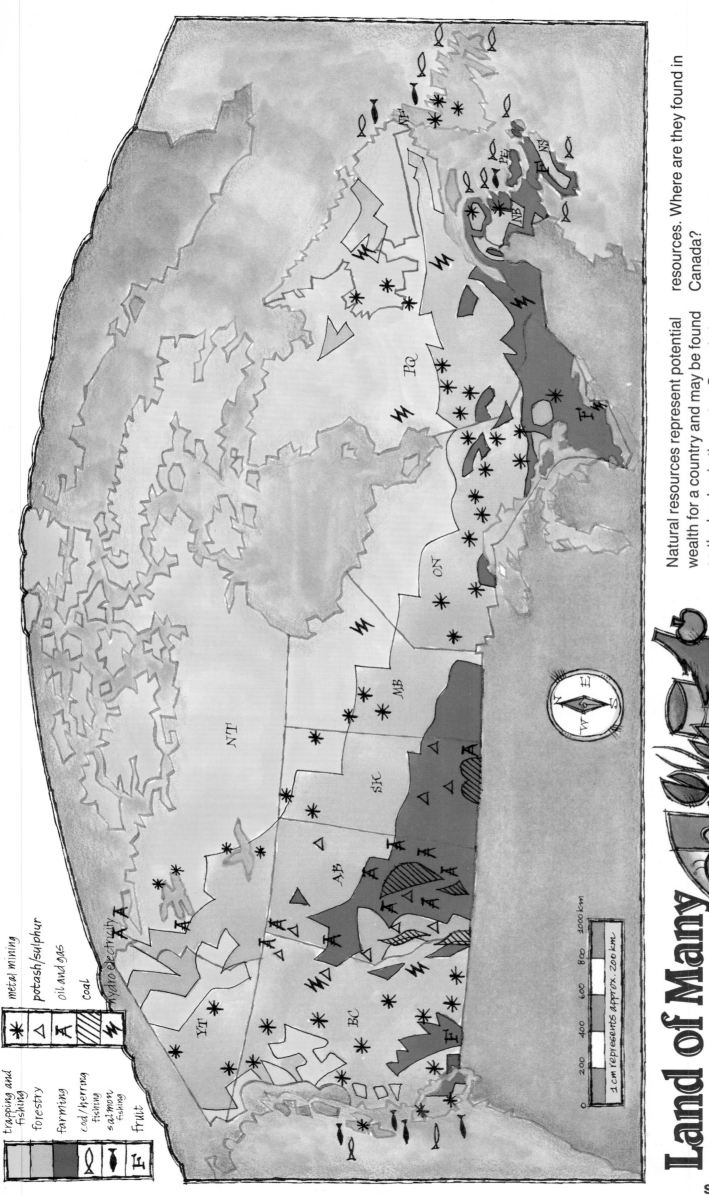

# Land of Many Resources

**Legend:**

| | |
|---|---|
| ✳ | metal mining |
| △ | potash/sulphur |
| Ă | oil and gas |
| ▨ | coal |
| ⋙ | hydro electricity |

| | |
|---|---|
| | trapping and fishing |
| | forestry |
| | farming |
| ⬠ | cod/herring fishing |
| ⬩ | salmon fishing |
| F | fruit |

Scale: 0 200 400 600 800 1000 km
1 cm represents approx. 200 km

Compass: N E S W

Provinces labelled: YT, BC, NT, AB, SK, MB, ON, PQ, NB, NS, PE, NF

Natural resources represent potential wealth for a country and may be found on the land or in the water. Canada has an abundance of natural resources. This map will help you to learn the locations of some of them. Canada needs lots of energy resources. Where are they found in Canada?

Describe the resources found in the province where you live.

Select one type of resource (such as metals) and produce a map for that resource.

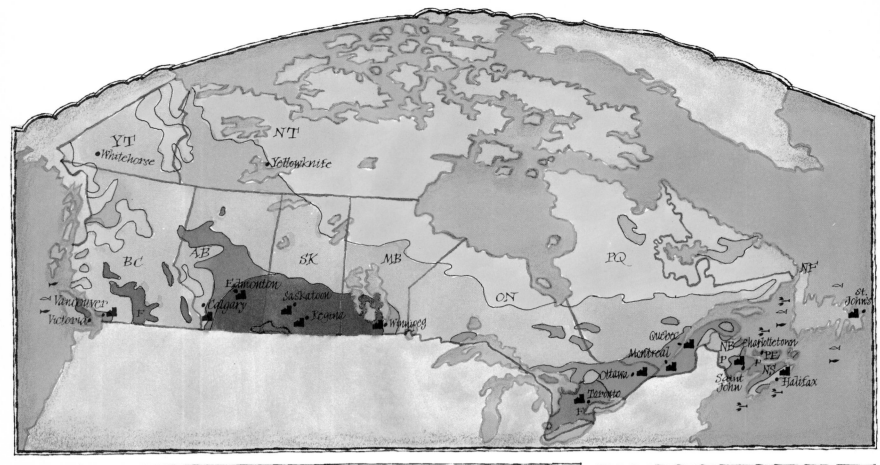

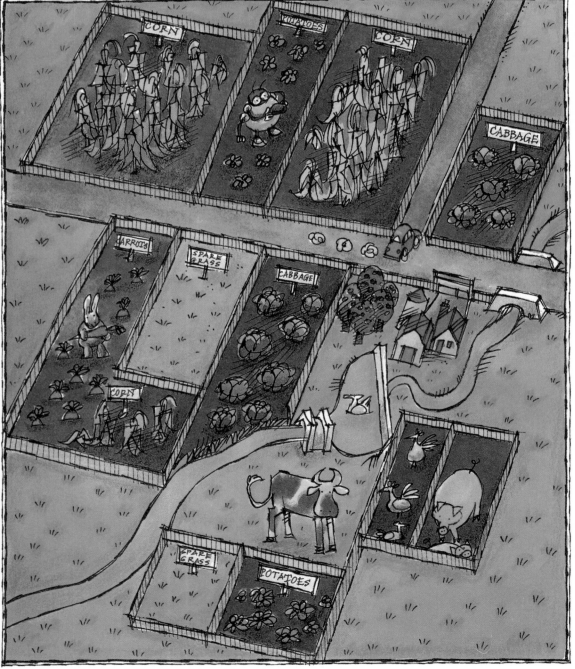

| trapping/fishing | F | fruit |
| forest | P | potatoes |
| animal grazing | cod/herring |
| mixed farming | salmon |
| grains | lobster |
| dairy farming | food processing centre |

# Land of Taste

Describe the types of food products that are found in the province where you live.

Which province is the most like yours in the kind of food it produces? Which is the most different?

What types of food cannot be grown in Canada? Why not? Use a resource centre to find five foods Canada sells to other countries and five foods it buys from other countries.

This is an oblique or slanting view of a farm. Prepare a map of the farm showing the view from above.

Three types of symbols have been used in this atlas: **point**, **line**, and **area**. What do you think is meant by each term? Give examples from pages you have studied.

Include each type of symbol on your map of the farm.

Give the farm a name and use this as the title for your map.

# Made in Canada

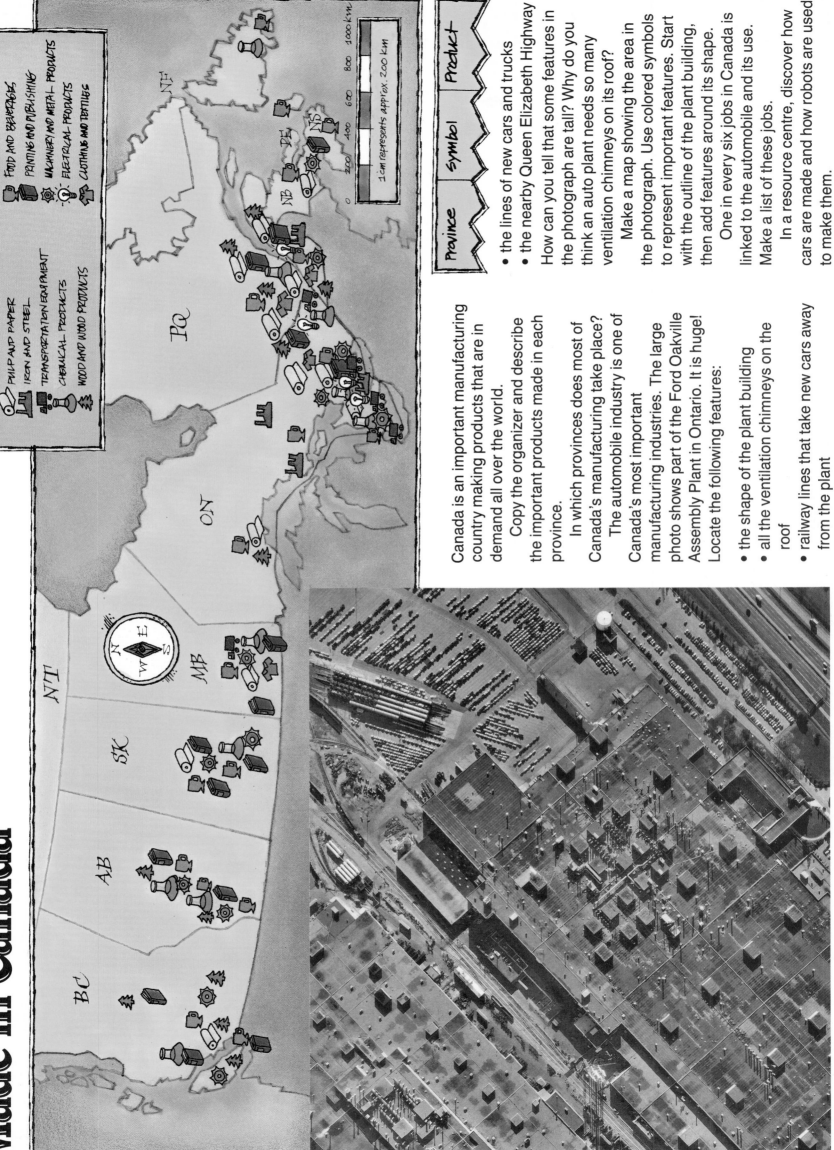

**Legend:**
- PULP AND PAPER
- IRON AND STEEL
- TRANSPORTATION EQUIPMENT
- CHEMICAL PRODUCTS
- WOOD AND WOOD PRODUCTS
- FOOD AND BEVERAGE
- PRINTING AND PUBLISHING
- MACHINERY AND METAL PRODUCTS
- ELECTRICAL PRODUCTS
- CLOTHING AND TEXTILES

Scale: 1 cm represents approx. 200 km
0 200 400 600 800 1000 km

Provinces: BC, AB, SK, MB, NT, ON, PQ, NF, NB, PE, NS

Canada is an important manufacturing country making products that are in demand all over the world.

Copy the organizer and describe the important products made in each province.

In which provinces does most of Canada's manufacturing take place?

The automobile industry is one of Canada's most important manufacturing industries. The large photo shows part of the Ford Oakville Assembly Plant in Ontario. It is huge! Locate the following features:

- the shape of the plant building
- all the ventilation chimneys on the roof
- railway lines that take new cars away from the plant
- the lines of new cars and trucks
- the nearby Queen Elizabeth Highway

How can you tell that some features in the photograph are tall? Why do you think an auto plant needs so many ventilation chimneys on its roof?

Make a map showing the area in the photograph. Use colored symbols to represent important features. Start with the outline of the plant building, then add features around its shape.

One in every six jobs in Canada is linked to the automobile and its use. Make a list of these jobs.

In a resource centre, discover how cars are made and how robots are used to make them.

| Province | Symbol | Product |
|----------|--------|---------|
|          |        |         |

# St. Lawrence Seaway

The St. Lawrence Seaway was opened on April 1, 1959 and is operated jointly by Canada and the United States. It allows St. Lawrence River ships and Atlantic Ocean ships at Montreal to navigate throughout the Great Lakes. Ships measuring up to 222.5 m long by 23.3 m wide with a depth of 7.9 m can pass through the 16 locks between Montreal and Lake Superior. Many of the "inland" ports on the Great Lakes handle as much cargo as ocean ports.

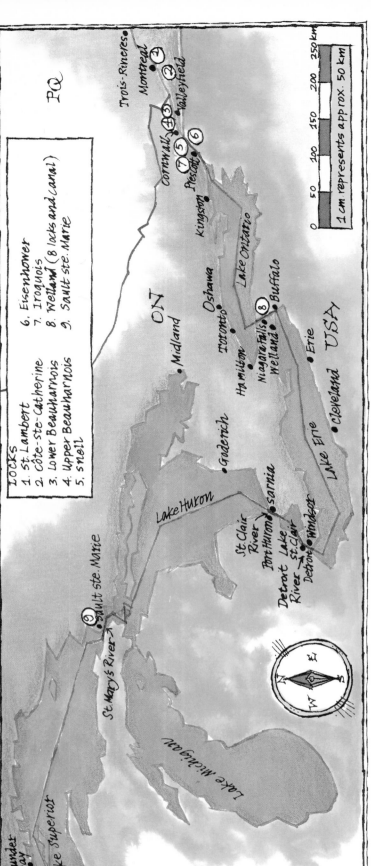

PQ

**Locks**
1. St. Lambert
2. Côte-ste-Catherine
3. Lower Beauharnois
4. Upper Beauharnois
5. Snell
6. Eisenhower
7. Iroquois
8. Welland (8 locks and canal)
9. Sault Ste. Marie

1 cm represents approx. 50 km

0   50   100   150   200   250 km

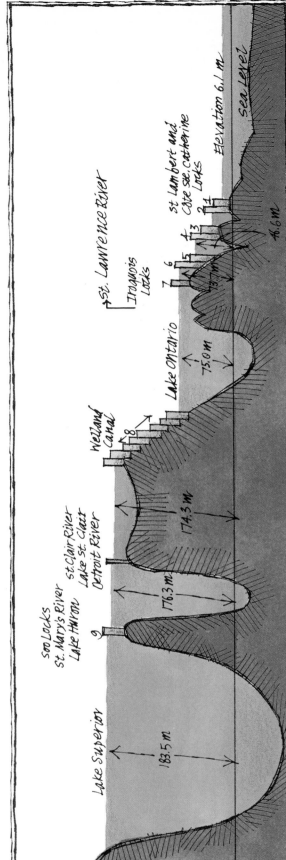

Sault Ste. Marie — Soo Locks
St. Mary's River
Lake Huron — St. Clair River
Lake St. Clair
Detroit River

Lake Superior    183.5 m

176.3 m

174.3 m

Welland Canal

Lake Ontario    75.0 m

Iroquois Locks    73.0 m

St. Lawrence River

St. Lambert and Côte Ste. Catherine Locks

Elevation 6.1 m

sea level

46.6 m

**Operation of a Lock**

Downstream gate open

Upstream gate closed

Drain valve open    Intake valve closed

Both gates closed as lock fills up

Drain valve closed    Intake valve open

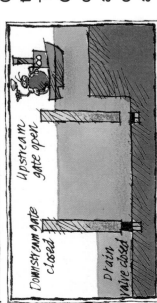

Downstream gate closed    Upstream gate open

Drain valve closed

You are the captain of a "laker"—a Great Lakes ship. You have been asked to take a cargo of Prairie wheat from Thunder Bay, Ontario, to Montreal, Quebec. There it will be loaded onto an ocean-going ship and delivered to another country. Sketch a rough drawing of your ship and give it a name and a logo. Then, complete a captain's

log in which you describe your journey along the border between Canada and the United States. Record the information for each category shown.

Create a map of the St. Lawrence Seaway that other ships' captains can use. Use symbols to show important places such as ports, canals, locks.

**Captain's log**
a) Lakes, rivers, canals used _____
b) Important cities along the route _____
c) Total distance travelled _____
d) Locks used _____
e) Drop in water level _____
f) Directions used _____

# Mainstreet Canada

Canada is said to have so many transportation routes along its southern edge, that it has a *mainstreet* along which its cities are located. Which cities are part of this *mainstreet*?

Some cities are important transportation centres because they have many different transportation routes radiating from them—like the spokes of a wheel. Which are Canada's important transportation cities?

You are sending a container full of globes from Halifax, Nova Scotia, to Edmonton, Alberta. You must

use each piece of container equipment shown in the top illustration. Write out a route plan that includes using the St. Lawrence Seaway between Quebec City and Thunder Bay.

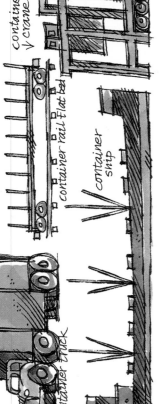

container V crane

container rail flat bed

container ship

container truck

**Legend**

- International Airport
- St. Lawrence Seaway
- Main Railway
- Trans-Canada Highway
- Other Main Roads
- Ferries

1 cm represents approx. 200 km

0  200  400  600  800  1000 km

# Today's Weather Report

You have been asked by your local television station to be the weather reporter for a day. Your first task is to make a map showing what the weather conditions across Canada are like. You are to use symbols to represent different types of weather.

Think of all the possible types of weather conditions (cloudy, sunny, etc.) and create a symbol for each type. Make a legend for your weather map.

Look at the sketches and figures on the map showing weather conditions across Canada. Using your symbols, draw a weather map for Canada showing these conditions.

Write a script for a two-minute weather report to be used on television. Describe the conditions across Canada and where you live.

# Environmental Challenge

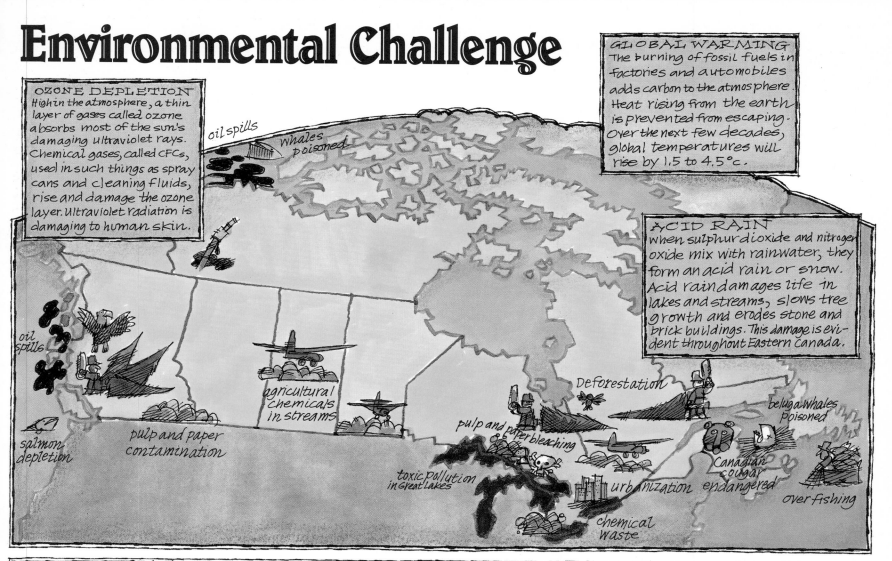

**OZONE DEPLETION**
High in the atmosphere, a thin layer of gases called ozone absorbs most of the sun's damaging ultraviolet rays. Chemical gases, called CFCs, used in such things as spray cans and cleaning fluids, rise and damage the ozone layer. Ultraviolet radiation is damaging to human skin.

**GLOBAL WARMING**
The burning of fossil fuels in factories and automobiles adds carbon to the atmosphere. Heat rising from the earth is prevented from escaping. Over the next few decades, global temperatures will rise by 1.5 to 4.5°C.

**ACID RAIN**
When sulphur dioxide and nitrogen oxide mix with rainwater, they form an acid rain or snow. Acid rain damages life in lakes and streams, slows tree growth and erodes stone and brick buildings. This damage is evident throughout Eastern Canada.

oil spills
whales poisoned
oil spills
salmon depletion
pulp and paper contamination
agricultural chemicals in streams
pulp and paper bleaching
toxic pollution in Great Lakes
chemical waste
urbanization
Deforestation
Canadian cougar endangered
beluga whales poisoned
over fishing

Congratulations! You are now an Environmental Protection Officer. Your first task is to clean up Sludgeville. You will need to create a map in order to see clearly where all the problems are to be found.

Prepare a legend for all the features you want on the map. Use the road as a line frame.

Make notes on the side of the map stating what the problems are and what needs to be done.

Write an environmental code of conduct that the people of Sludgeville should follow in order to make their community better. Suggest a new name for the community to reflect its new image.

# Continental Sportivities

Make a map which shows where some professional sports teams are located. Use the steps below as a guideline.

- Trace the outline of the map of North America.
- Create a symbol to represent each of the professional sports listed.
- Draw the symbol that represents the professional sport near the location where the sport is played. Some locations will have a number of symbols around them.

From the teams shown on the map, select your favorite. What is the furthest distance that team will have to travel to play another team in its league and which is also shown on the map?

For one of the professional sports, do some research to identify the rest of the teams in the league. Make a list and then draw a map for that sport.

Choose a sport that does not have a professional league, such as volleyball, surfing, ringette, skiing.

- Select eight cities where teams will form a league for that sport.
- Create a name for each team.
- Draw a map for your league.

Select one team from your league.

- Design a team logo.
- Prepare a playing schedule where you play each of the other teams in the league twice.
- Estimate the total travelling distance for your team.

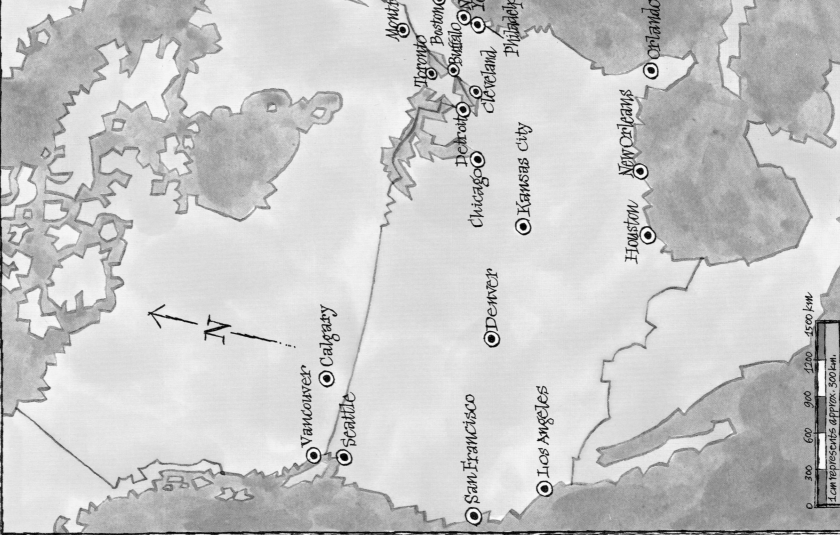

1 cm represents approx. 300 km.
0  300  600  900  1200  1500 km

## Selected Professional Sports Cities

| | ICE HOCKEY | FOOT-BALL | SOCCER | BASE-BALL | BASKET-BALL |
|---|---|---|---|---|---|
| Vancouver | ● | | ● | | |
| Calgary | ● | ● | | | |
| Toronto | ● | ● | ● | ● | |
| Montreal | ● | ● | | ● | |
| Buffalo | ● | ● | | | |
| Boston | ● | | | ● | ● |
| New York | ● | ● | | ● | ● |
| Philadelphia | ● | ● | | ● | ● |
| Chicago | ● | ● | ● | ● | ● |
| Detroit | ● | ● | | ● | ● |
| Cleveland | | ● | | ● | ● |
| Kansas City | | ● | | ● | |
| Denver | ● | ● | | | ● |
| Houston | | ● | | ● | ● |
| New Orleans | | ● | | | |
| Orlando | | | | | ● |
| Los Angeles | ● | ● | ● | ● | ● |
| San Francisco | | ● | | ● | ● |
| Seattle | | ● | | ● | ● |

# Where Is It?

If you were asked where Ottawa is, you might know the answer without having to look at a map because it is the capital of Canada and is often featured in news reports. If, however, you were asked where Reindeer Lake is, the chances are you would not know unless you lived in northern Saskatchewan.

There will be many occasions when you will want to find out by looking at an atlas where a certain place is located.

Where will you be going on your summer vacation? Do you know where it is located? Do you have a pen pal? Where does he or she live? Do you know where that is on a map?

A **gazetteer** is found at the back of an atlas. It is a dictionary or index of places or features which appear in the atlas. Following the name is the page number where you will find a map showing that place or feature, and the grid reference to help you locate it on the map.

You will find a gazetteer at the end of this atlas for most of the place names and features which appear on pages 56 to 67. For example:

- Wolfville, Nova Scotia, is found on page 59 in grid reference C2.

- The country of Papua New Guinea is located on page 67 in grid reference P5.

Use the gazetteer to find the following places:

- North Bay, Ontario
- Oshawa, Ontario
- Kelowna, British Columbia
- Yellowknife, Northwest Territories

What do they each have in common? Prepare three questions to ask someone about places in this atlas. Give them only the gazetteer reference as a clue.

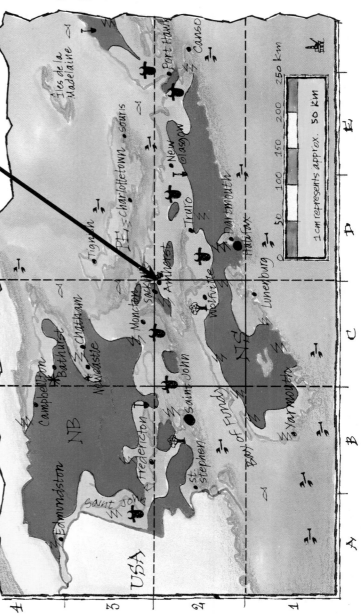

# Pacific Canada

You are helping to prepare the information which is to appear in the gazetteer. Select five places in British Columbia, list them in alphabetical order, and show the page number and grid reference for each.

Check your answer against the gazetteer at the back of this atlas.

Use a resource centre to research what it is really like. Make a list of things you find *most* interesting about this province. What are the major industries?

What images come to mind when you think of British Columbia?

If you were taking a trip to British Columbia, which places would you like to visit? Why? What are the grid references for those places?

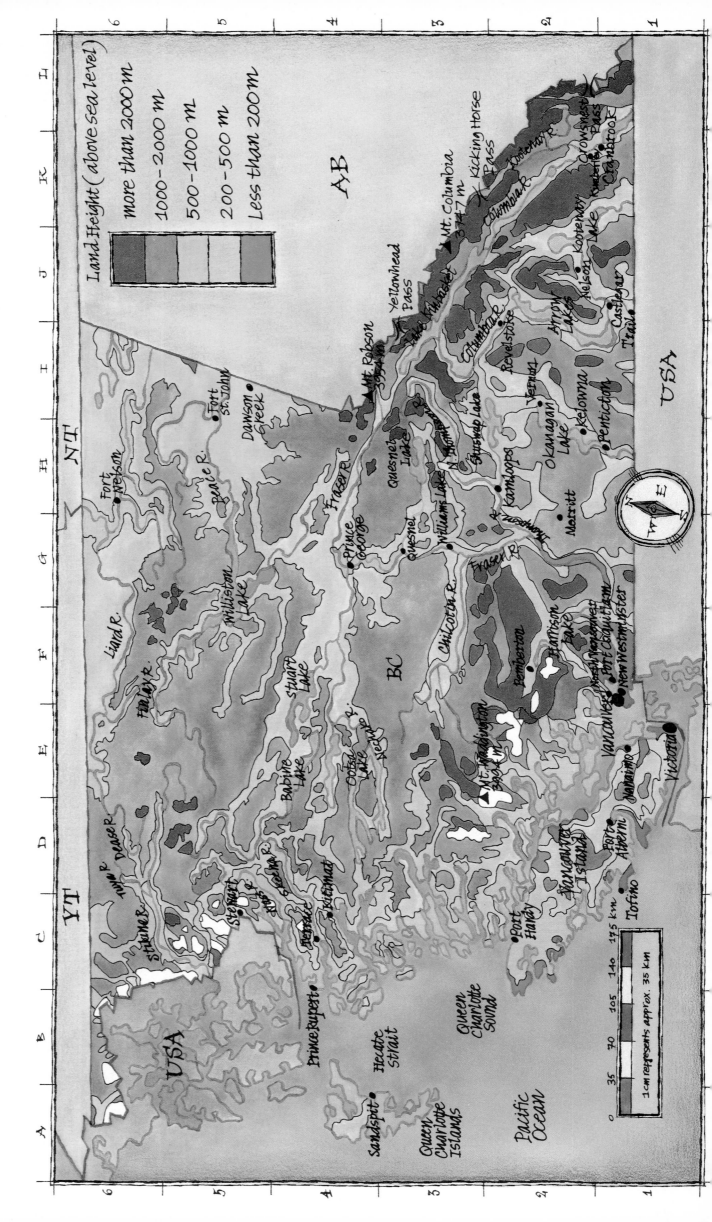

Land Height (above sea level)

- more than 2000 m
- 1000 - 2000 m
- 500 - 1000 m
- 200 - 500 m
- Less than 200 m

1 cm represents approx. 35 km

0  35  70  105  140  175 km

# Vancouver

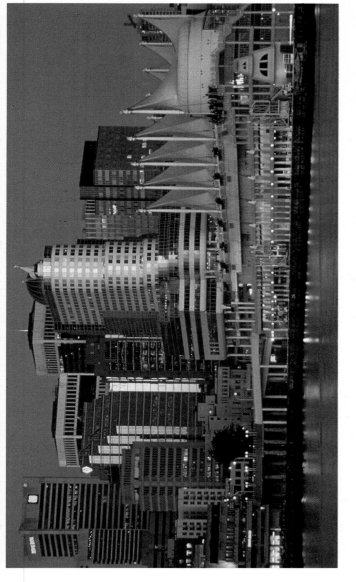

Vancouver is one of the most beautiful cities in Canada. Located on coastal lowland between snow capped mountains and the Pacific Ocean, it is British Columbia's largest city.

Here are some views of downtown Vancouver. One view is an aerial photograph which changes towering skyscrapers into simple shapes. Another is an oblique map (not quite vertical) in which you can see the height of the buildings and features.

With the oblique map to help you, identify the places marked by letters on the aerial photograph.

Using the map and the aerial photograph, identify some of the buildings shown in the photograph on the right.

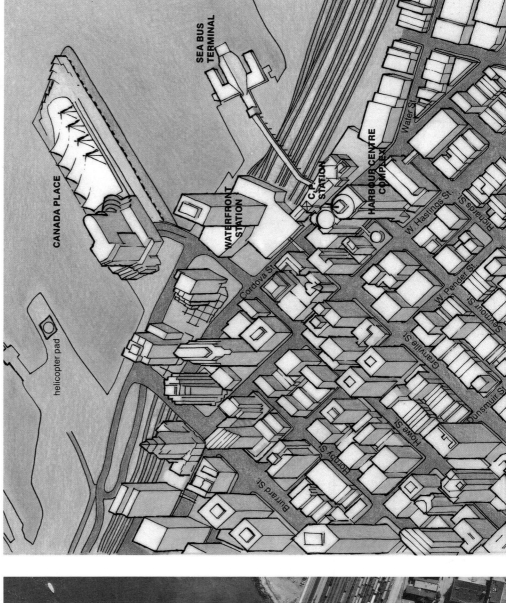

# Prairies Canada

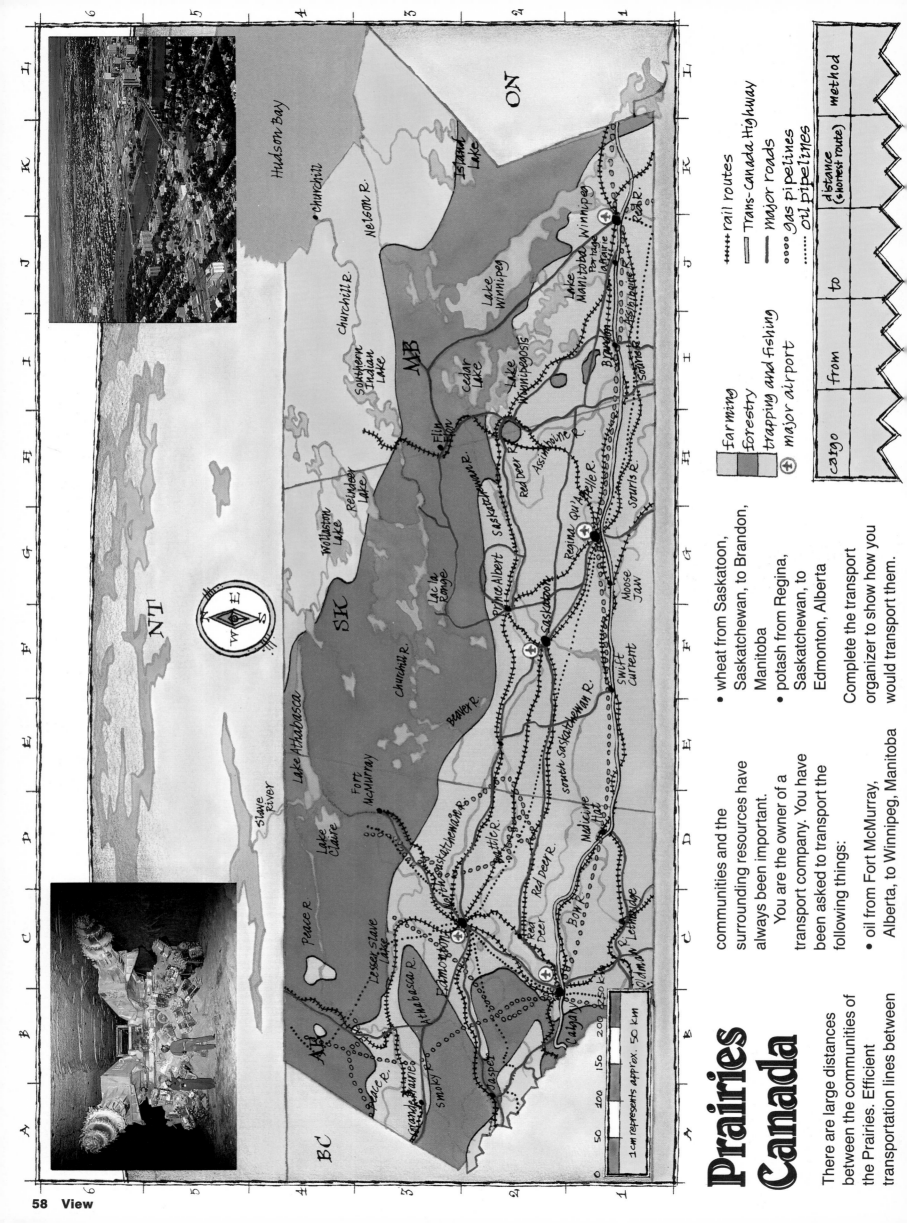

**Legend:**
- ++++ rail routes
- ═══ Trans-Canada Highway
- —— major roads
- ∘∘∘ gas pipelines
- ······ oil pipelines

| | |
|---|---|
| ▨ farming | |
| ▨ forestry | |
| ▨ trapping and fishing | |
| ✈ major airport | |

| cargo | from | to | distance (shortest route) | method |
|---|---|---|---|---|
| | | | | |
| | | | | |
| | | | | |
| | | | | |

**Map labels:** NT, BC, AB, SK, MB, ON, Hudson Bay, Churchill, Nelson R., Churchill R., Southern Indian Lake, Lake Winnipeg, Cedar Lake, Lake Winnipegosis, Lake Manitoba, Winnipeg, Portage la Prairie, Red R., Brandon, Assiniboine R., Souris R., Qu'Appelle R., Regina, Moose Jaw, Saskatchewan R., Prince Albert, Flin Flon, Reindeer Lake, Wollaston Lake, Lac la Ronge, Beaver R., Churchill R., Saskatoon, South Saskatchewan R., Swift Current, Medicine Hat, Souris R., Battle R., North Saskatchewan R., Red Deer R., Bow R., Oldman R., Lethbridge, Calgary, Red Deer, Edmonton, Lesser Slave Lake, Athabasca R., Smoky R., Peace R., Jasper, Grande Prairie, Beaver R., Lake Claire, Lake Athabasca, Fort McMurray, Slave River

**Scale:** 1 cm represents approx. 50 km — 50 100 150 200 250 km

There are large distances between the communities of the Prairies. Efficient transportation lines between communities and the surrounding resources have always been important.

You are the owner of a transport company. You have been asked to transport the following things:

- oil from Fort McMurray, Alberta, to Winnipeg, Manitoba
- wheat from Saskatoon, Saskatchewan, to Brandon, Manitoba
- potash from Regina, Saskatchewan, to Edmonton, Alberta

Complete the transport organizer to show how you would transport them.

# Atlantic Canada

Atlantic Canada provides an abundance of resources from the land and the sea.

Use an organizer to make a list of work people do that involves taking something out of the ground or ocean (e.g. drilling for oil and gas).

Which of the resources are **renewable** (will replace themselves)?

Which are **non-renewable** (will not replace themselves)?

You are the captain of a fishing trawler from Lunenburg. Large amounts of fish have been spotted in grid references **H2**, **H5** and **J3**. Plan a route that will enable you to fish in each place. Using the line scale, estimate the approximate distance you would have to travel.

Use the drawing of a fishing trawler to design a ship that will be named by you. Label all parts of the trawler.

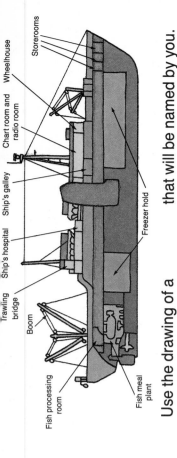

Wheelhouse
Storerooms
Chart room and radio room
Ship's galley
Ship's hospital
Trawling bridge
Boom
Fish processing room
Fish meal plant
Freezer hold

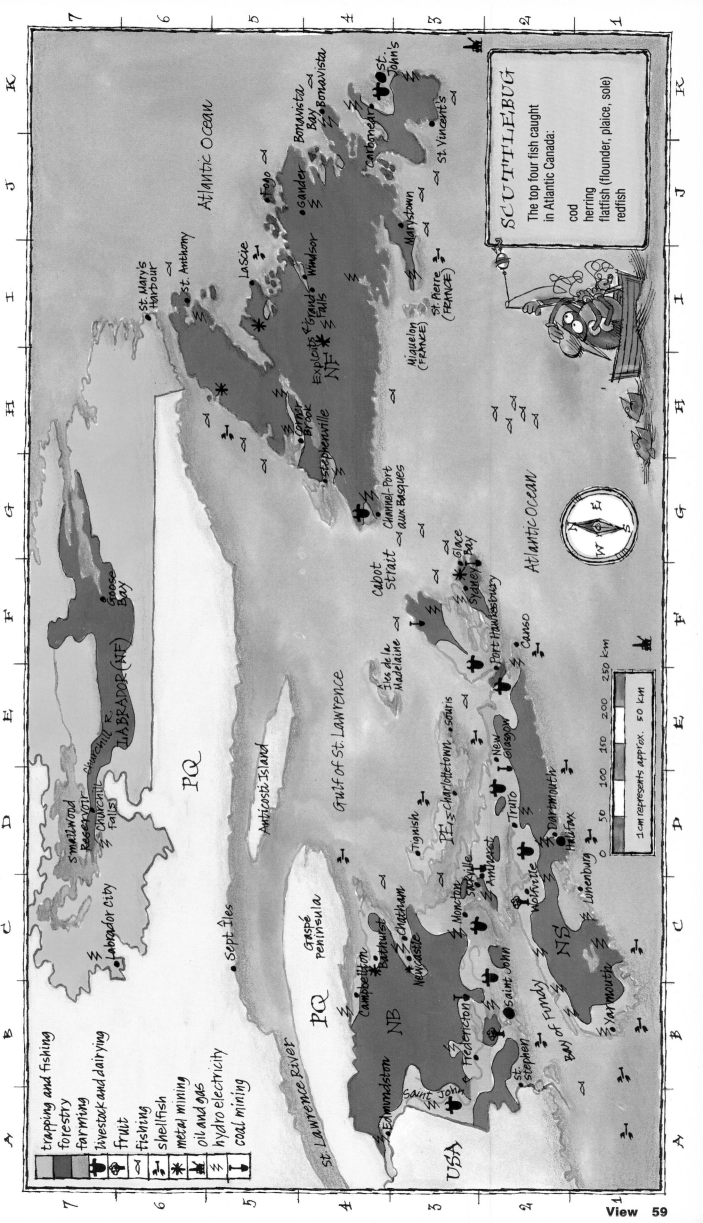

trapping and fishing
forestry
farming
livestock and dairying
fruit
fishing
shellfish
metal mining
oil and gas
hydro electricity
coal mining

SCUTTLEBUG

The top four fish caught in Atlantic Canada:

cod
herring
flatfish (flounder, plaice, sole)
redfish

1 cm represents approx. 50 km

0   50   100   150   200   250 km

# Central Canada

Create an organizer for central Canada using the headings *City* and *Industry*. Describe the industries found in some of the cities of central Canada.

Create a symbol to represent the industries in the following cities: Niagara, Oshawa, Hamilton, Sudbury.

Draw a map of this area and use your symbols to illustrate the industries for each city.

If you were able to have a summer job in one of these cities, where would you like to work? Why?

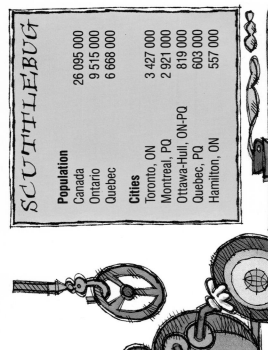

| CENTRAL CANADA | |
|---|---|
| City | Industry |
| | |

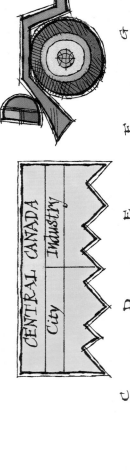

**SCUTTLEBUG**

**Population**

| | |
|---|---|
| Canada | 26 095 000 |
| Ontario | 9 515 000 |
| Quebec | 6 668 000 |

**Cities**

| | |
|---|---|
| Toronto, ON | 3 427 000 |
| Montreal, PQ | 2 921 000 |
| Ottawa-Hull, ON-PQ | 819 000 |
| Quebec, PQ | 603 000 |
| Hamilton, ON | 557 000 |

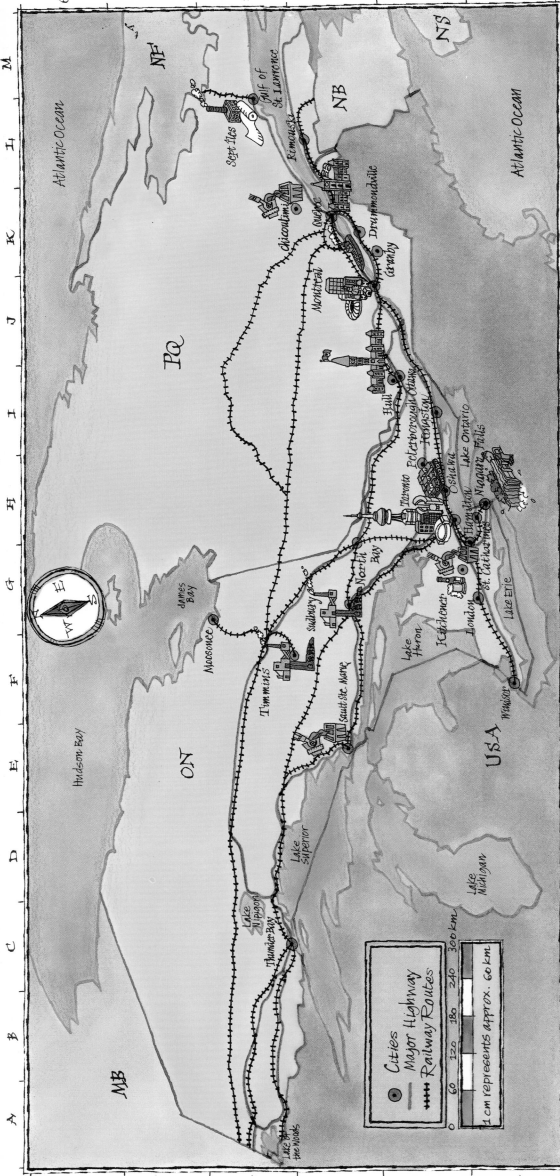

# Toronto

Welcome to Toronto! Pinned on the map is a list of places you want to visit. Your starting point is at the intersection of Queen Street and Yonge Street.

Prepare an organizer using the headings *Place to Visit* and *Route Taken*. In the left column list each place in the order that you will visit it. In the right column give the directions from the previous place.

Now it is raining and cold. Use the underground walkway shown in the map on the right. Visit the same places as before and describe your route below the streets and buildings.

You have one picture left to take with your camera. Write a description of the picture you will take.

map of underground walkway

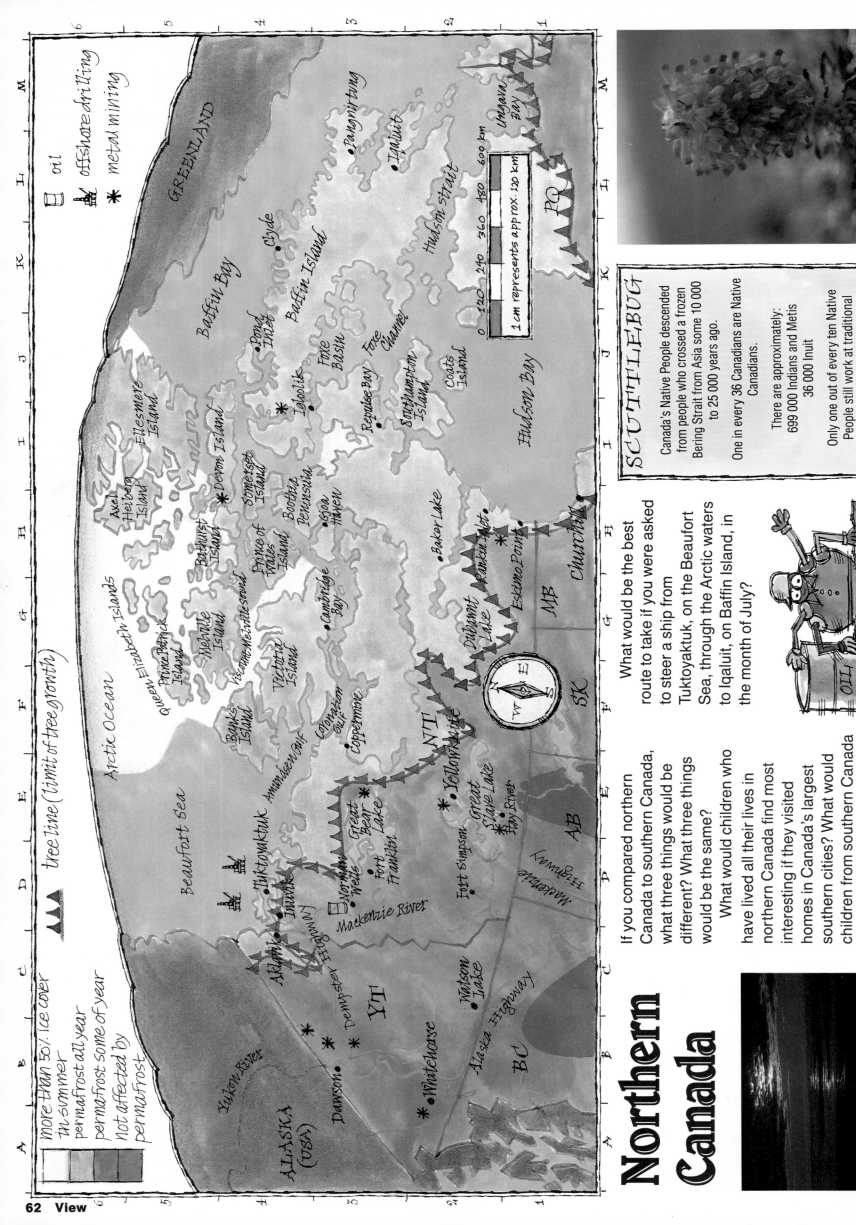

# Northern Canada

If you compared northern Canada to southern Canada, what three things would be different? What three things would be the same?

What would children who have lived all their lives in northern Canada find most interesting if they visited homes in Canada's largest southern cities? What would children from southern Canada find interesting about northern homes?

What would be the best route to take if you were asked to steer a ship from Tuktoyaktuk, on the Beaufort Sea, through the Arctic waters to Iqaluit, on Baffin Island, in the month of July?

## SCUTTLEBUG

Canada's Native People descended from people who crossed a frozen Bering Strait from Asia some 10 000 to 25 000 years ago.

One in every 36 Canadians are Native Canadians.

There are approximately: 699 000 Indians and Metis 36 000 Inuit

Only one out of every ten Native People still work at traditional hunting, trapping and fishing.

# Different Places— Different Views

Each of these four maps has been drawn as if you were looking at a view of the rest of Canada from the following places:

1. Coppermine, Northwest Territories
2. Windsor, Ontario
3. St. John's, Newfoundland
4. Victoria, British Columbia

Use maps from other pages in this atlas to compare them to the views shown on this page.

If you were living in the following places, which of the four maps would be similar to your view of Canada?

• Hamilton, Ontario (looking northwards)

• Halifax, Nova Scotia (looking westwards)
• Calgary, Alberta (looking eastwards)
• Tuktoyaktuk (looking southwards)

Trace one of the maps and label some of the water bodies and land features. Show the location of your community.

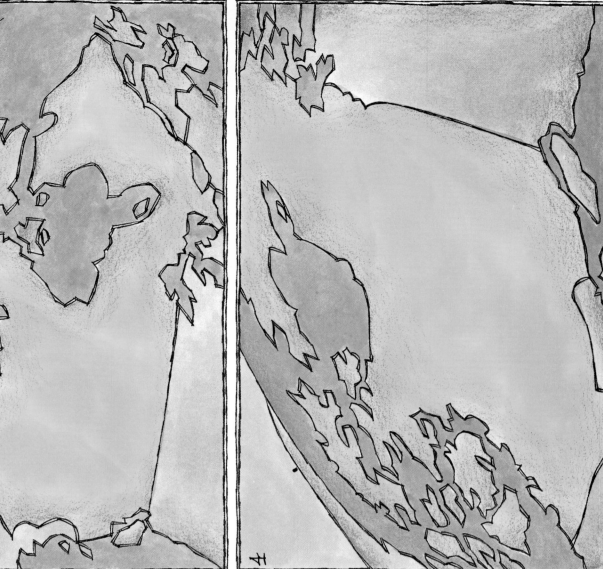

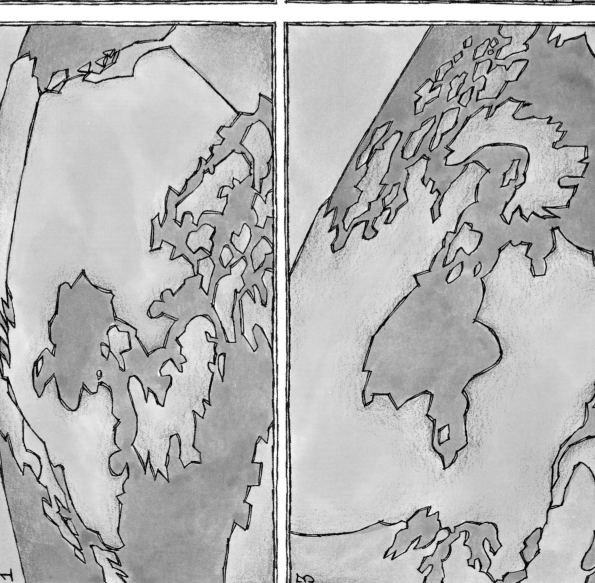

# Pacific Rim

From Vancouver, British Columbia, you are to deliver a cargo of items to two Pacific Rim countries and then return with a cargo of goods for Canada.

Select two countries. What items do they purchase from Canada? What items does Canada purchase from them?

Complete the captain's log. Repeat the exercise with voyages to four other destinations.

| starting port | cargo | destination | direction | distance |
|---|---|---|---|---|
| | | | | |

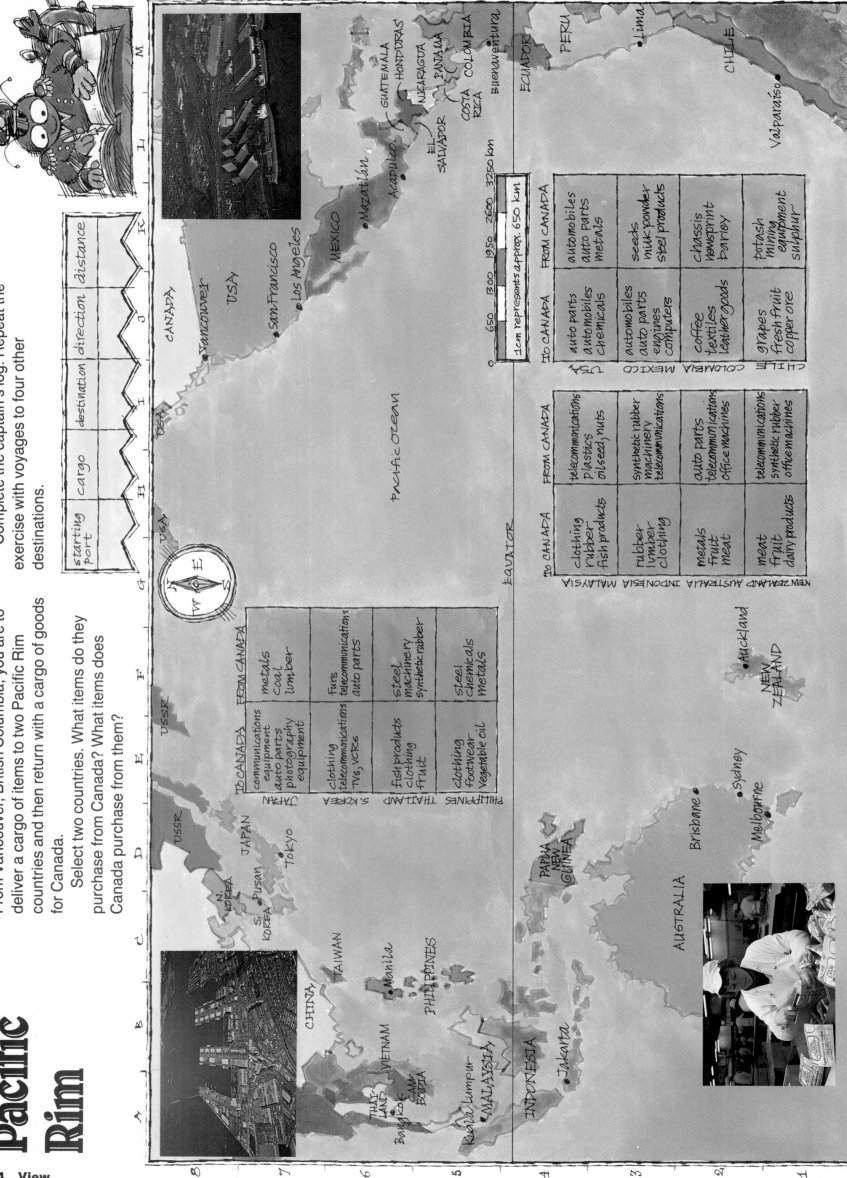

Pacific Ocean

EQUATOR

1cm represents approx. 650 km

0  650  1300  1950  2600  3250 km

| | TO CANADA | FROM CANADA |
|---|---|---|
| JAPAN | communications equipment auto parts photography equipment | metals coal lumber |
| S. KOREA | clothing telecommunications TVs, VCRs | furs telecommunications auto parts |
| THAILAND | fish products clothing fruit | steel machinery synthetic rubber |
| PHILIPPINES | clothing footwear vegetable oil | steel chemicals metals |

| | TO CANADA | FROM CANADA |
|---|---|---|
| USA | auto parts automobiles chemicals | automobiles auto parts metals |
| MEXICO | automobiles auto parts engines computers | seeds milk powder steel products |
| COLOMBIA | coffee textiles leather goods | chassis newsprint barley |
| CHILE | grapes fresh fruit copper ore | potash mining equipment sulphur |

| | TO CANADA | FROM CANADA |
|---|---|---|
| NEW ZEALAND | clothing rubber fish products | telecommunications plastics oilseed, nuts |
| AUSTRALIA | rubber lumber clothing | synthetic rubber machinery telecommunications |
| INDONESIA | metals fruit meat | auto parts telecommunications office machines |
| MALAYSIA | meat fruit dairy products | telecommunications synthetic rubber office machines |

# Atlantic
# Links

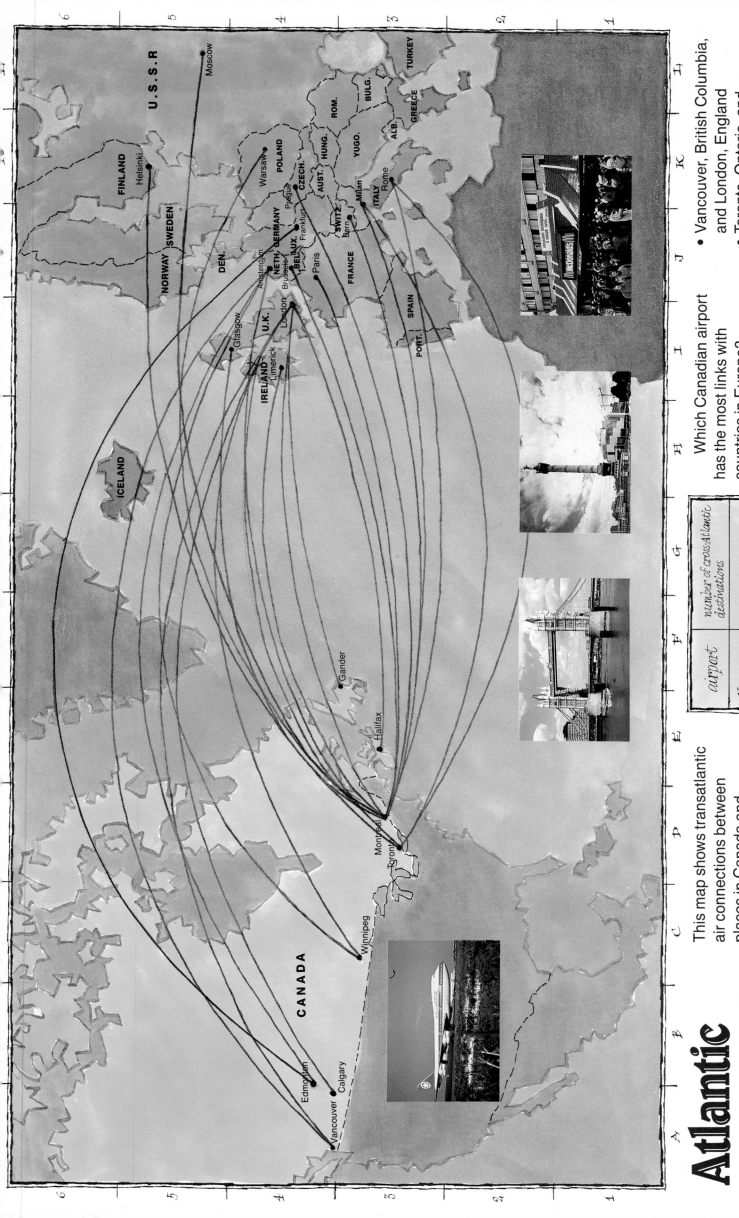

This map shows transatlantic air connections between places in Canada and destinations in other countries.

Complete the organizer to show the number of flights that cross the Atlantic Ocean from Canadian airports.

Which Canadian airport has the most links with countries in Europe?

Which is the furthest direct flight?

Use a piece of string on a globe to find the direction of the shortest flight between the following places:

- Vancouver, British Columbia, and London, England
- Toronto, Ontario, and Moscow, USSR

Use the line scale on the globe and the piece of string to find the approximate distances of each direct flight.

| airport | number of cross-Atlantic destinations |
|---|---|
| Vancouver | |
| Edmonton | |
| Calgary | |
| Winnipeg | |
| Toronto | |
| Montreal | |
| Halifax | |
| Gander | |

# Canada and the World

Plan a trip around the world that includes visiting at least one country on each continent. Record your trip in the organizer shown.

For one of the countries visited, discover more information about it in a resource centre. Look for ways in which that country is both *similar to* and *different from* Canada.

Visit a resource centre. Create a data base of countries and their capital cities.

| country visited | distance from previous stop | direction travelled |
|---|---|---|
| | | |

A    B    C    D    E    F    G

| | | |
|---|---|---|
| 1 | BELIZE | 25 | BHUTAN |
| 2 | JAMAICA | 26 | BANGLADESH |
| 3 | HAITI | 27 | THAILAND |
| 4 | PUERTO RICO | 28 | CAMBODIA |
| 5 | TRINIDAD AND TOBAGO | 29 | BRUNEI |
| 6 | NETHERLANDS | 30 | THE GAMBIA |
| 7 | BELGIUM | 31 | GUINEA-BISSAU |
| 8 | GERMANY | 32 | SIERRA LEONE |
| 9 | CZECHOSLOVAKIA | 33 | BURKINO FASO |
| 10 | AUSTRIA | 34 | TOGO |
| 11 | YUGOSLAVIA | 35 | BENIN |
| 12 | HUNGARY | 36 | EQUATORIAL GUINEA |
| 13 | ROMANIA | 37 | CENTRAL AFRICAN REPUBLIC |
| 14 | BULGARIA | 38 | UGANDA |
| 15 | ALBANIA | 39 | RWANDA |
| 16 | SWITZERLAND | 40 | BURUNDI |
| 17 | SYRIA | 41 | MALAWI |
| 18 | LEBANON | 42 | ZIMBABWE |
| 19 | ISRAEL | 43 | BOTSWANA |
| 20 | JORDAN | 44 | SWAZILAND |
| 21 | KUWAIT | 45 | LESOTHO |
| 22 | BAHRAIN | | |
| 23 | QATAR | | |
| 24 | UNITED ARAB EMIRATES | | |

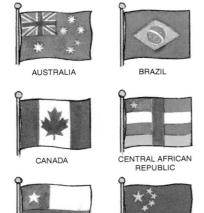

AUSTRALIA    BRAZIL

CANADA    CENTRAL AFRICAN REPUBLIC

CHILE    CHINA

COLOMBIA    CUBA

FRANCE    GREECE

GUINEA-BISSAU    INDIA

IRAN    IRAQ

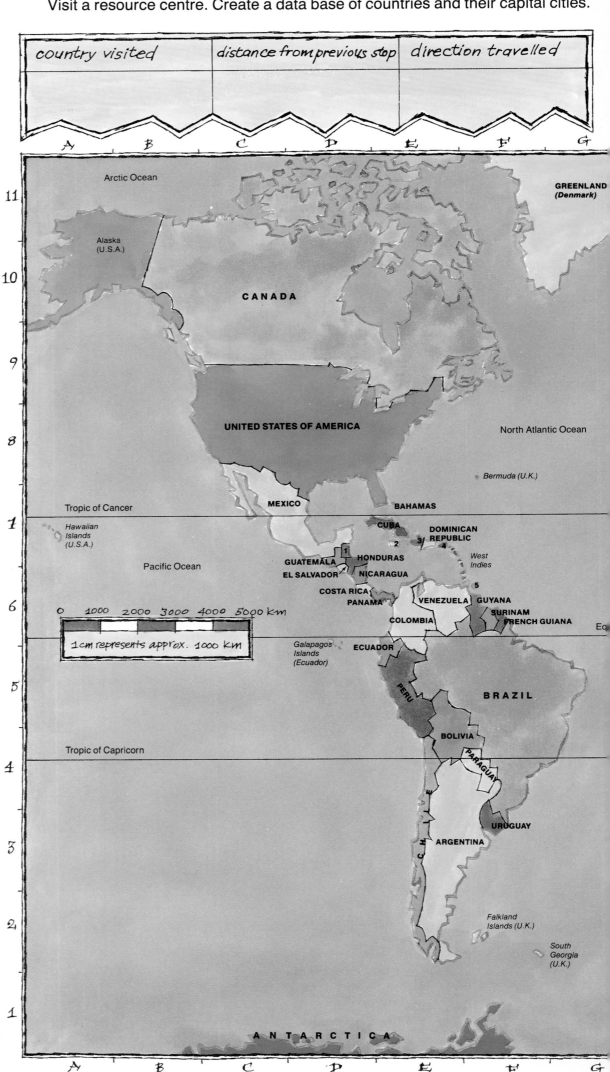

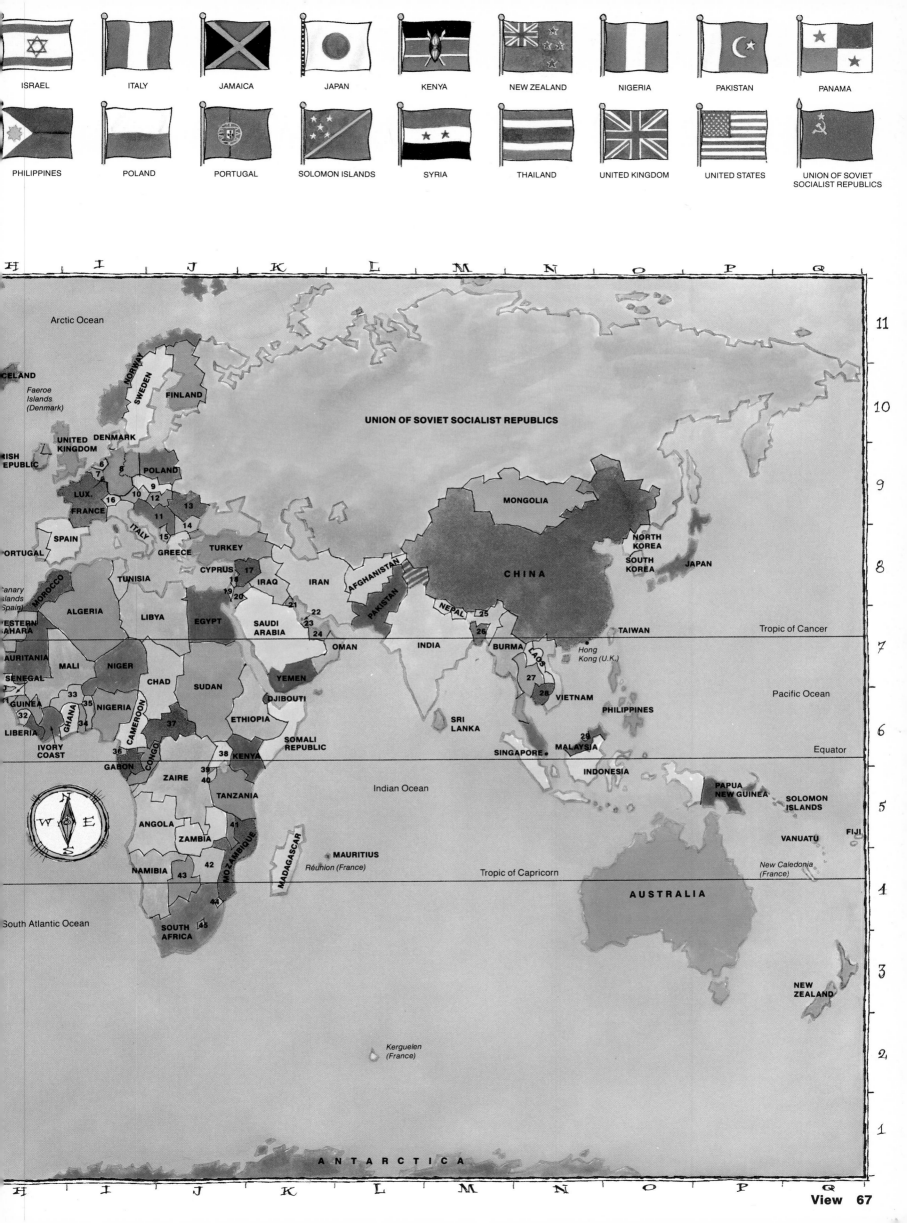

ISRAEL    ITALY    JAMAICA    JAPAN    KENYA    NEW ZEALAND    NIGERIA    PAKISTAN    PANAMA

PHILIPPINES    POLAND    PORTUGAL    SOLOMON ISLANDS    SYRIA    THAILAND    UNITED KINGDOM    UNITED STATES    UNION OF SOVIET SOCIALIST REPUBLICS

Arctic Ocean

ICELAND
Faeroe Islands (Denmark)
IRISH REPUBLIC
UNITED KINGDOM
DENMARK
NORWAY
SWEDEN
FINLAND

UNION OF SOVIET SOCIALIST REPUBLICS

6
7
8
POLAND
LUX.
16
10
12
13
FRANCE
11
14
15
PORTUGAL
SPAIN
ITALY
GREECE
TURKEY
CYPRUS
17
18
19
20
IRAQ
IRAN
AFGHANISTAN
MONGOLIA
NORTH KOREA
SOUTH KOREA
JAPAN
CHINA
Canary Islands (Spain)
MOROCCO
WESTERN SAHARA
TUNISIA
ALGERIA
LIBYA
EGYPT
SAUDI ARABIA
21
22
23
24
OMAN
PAKISTAN
NEPAL
25
INDIA
26
BURMA
LAOS
TAIWAN
Hong Kong (U.K.)
Tropic of Cancer
MAURITANIA
MALI
NIGER
CHAD
SUDAN
33
35
NIGERIA
CAMEROON
34
GHANA
36
CONGO
37
ETHIOPIA
YEMEN
DJIBOUTI
SOMALI REPUBLIC
SRI LANKA
27
28
VIETNAM
PHILIPPINES
SINGAPORE
29
MALAYSIA
Pacific Ocean
SENEGAL
GUINEA
32
LIBERIA
IVORY COAST
GABON
38
KENYA
ZAIRE
39
40
TANZANIA
Equator
INDONESIA
PAPUA NEW GUINEA
SOLOMON ISLANDS
Indian Ocean
ANGOLA
ZAMBIA
41
MOZAMBIQUE
MADAGASCAR
MAURITIUS
Réunion (France)
VANUATU
FIJI
New Caledonia (France)
NAMIBIA
42
43
Tropic of Capricorn
AUSTRALIA
44
South Atlantic Ocean
SOUTH AFRICA
45
Kerguelen (France)
NEW ZEALAND
A N T A R C T I C A

# Gazetteer